MARINER'S COMPASS

AN AMERICAN QUILT CLASSIC

Judy Mathieson

C & T Publishing
Lafayette, California

Front Cover Photo:
Center Detail from *Nautical Stars,*
Judy Mathieson, 1986

Copyright © 1987 by Judy Mathieson

Photography by Jack Mathieson
Woodland Hills, CA

Illustrations by Helen Young Frost
Sunland, CA

Design/Production Coordination by Bobbi Sloan Design
Berkeley, CA

Typesetting by Archetype
Berkeley, CA

Published by
C&T Publishing
P.O. Box 1456
Lafayette, CA 94549

ISBN: 0-914881-11-6

Library of Congress Catalog Card No: 87-71884

Printed in the United States of America

Contents

Compass Rose from Wind Roses quilt.

Foreword

Old quilt block, 1830–1840.

Mariner's Compass, one of the oldest quilt block designs used in the United States, has the reputation of being a difficult pattern. When I first became interested in making quilts, I had no family quilting background and only one reference book, *The Standard Book of Quiltmaking and Collecting* by Marguerite Ickes. I went through the book selecting designs that interested me, and since I had no one to tell me to start simple and work up, I made what appealed to me, a Mariner's Compass. As I look at that block now, it went together just fine. While the points don't all touch the outer circle, they *are* pointy and the block lies flat. This is not to imply that I was a natural quiltmaker, as my first try at appliqué had quickly ended up in the wastebasket.

When I joined the national community of quiltmakers, I discovered that many people considered the Mariner's Compass block so hard and complex that they put off making it until their skills had improved. I had instant status just because I had successfully pieced a Mariner's Compass. So you, too, can be thought of as a skilled quiltmaker. It's true that the Mariner's Compass block requires attention to detail—you can't be sloppy—but most of the sewing is straight lines with no set-in corners. Many Mariner's Compass designs are completed with an appliqué circle in the middle so you don't even have to deal with eight seams coming together.

Mary Hudson of San Juan Bautista, California, organized a group quilt in 1986 (Color Plate 11) using one of the designs included in this book. She reports that several of her friends had only made one or two quilt blocks before and still had no problems with this rather complex Mariner's Compass.

This book offers patterns for some simple styles as well as more complex designs. "Do what I say and not what I do" and start with the simpler ones. If you find that the patterns in this book are not the right size for the quilt you have in mind, try the chapter on drafting your own Mariner's Compass. Do you have a picture of an old compass quilt that you would like to reproduce or perhaps a wonderful compass rose from a navigational chart that inspires you? Try drafting it yourself. Don't be afraid of graph paper and the drafting compass. They are tools for the quiltmaker just as knives and thermometers are for the cook.

During the last ten years, there has been an explosion of publications on quiltmaking. This book, intended to appeal to the quiltmaker past the beginning stage, does not cover basic information about quiltmaking. Recommended books on beginning quiltmaking are listed in the bibliography. If you have limited experience in quiltmaking, try your public library as well as your local bookstore for introductory books. Probably the best sources for books on quiltmaking are the advertisements in the quilting periodicals; several of these magazines are listed in the bibliography.

My thanks to Esther Barnwell, Jane Blair, Vera Cummings, Brenda Glyn-Williams, Mary Hudson, Linda Otto Lipsett, Danita Rafalovich, and Linda Wolfard who trusted me with their quilts, and to Jinny Beyer, Rod Kiracofe, Cyril I. Nelson, Julie Silber, Linda Reuther, and the Shelburne Museum who gave permission to use their photographs. Special thanks to my husband, Jack, for his patience, photography and technical assistance. I am also grateful to Barbara Brackman, Roberta Horton, Adele Ingraham, Mary Mashuta, Pat Scoville, and all the other quilting friends who supported me in this effort.

Compass Rose from 16th-century map.

Introduction

A circle with radiating points occurs as a design in most cultures. It represents many things and may be called a star, sunburst, or, on a navigational chart or map where it indicates direction, a compass. Before the magnetic compass came into general use in the 13th century, sailors in the Mediterranean used eight predictable winds to navigate. These eight winds were represented on charts or maps by a design called a wind rose. As the magnetic compass became common, its northern point was superimposed on the design and became a compass card or compass rose. When the design made its way to the quilt block, it became known as Mariner's Compass.

Quilt historian Barbara Brackman lists the Mariner's Compass design as originating very early, perhaps by the first quarter of the 19th century. It is certainly true that quilt-makers along the eastern seaboard of the United States had access to maps and navigational charts that showed compass roses. Perhaps they would have called these quilts Mariner's Compass, but we will never know for sure.

If you search the quilt literature and published patterns of the last fifty years, the names of these designs are most often sunburst, sunflower, or star. What's the difference? Carter Houck speculates in *American Quilts and How To Make Them* that the difference might be in the technique. Mariner's Compass patterns seem to be pieced with pie-shaped wedges into circles, while the others seem to be executed in appliqué (no wonder those points aren't pointy). However, it also follows that quiltmakers who didn't live near a large body of water would be more apt to relate to a familiar name like sunburst or sunflower than to Mariner's Compass.

A quilt pattern should probably be called Mariner's Compass only when it has 32 points or some division of that number, like a compass card with its 32 points. However, in this book I will refer to all the designs as Mariner's Compass and indicate the type of variation with a descriptive name, e.g., split, sunburst, sunflower, concentric circle, or by the basic numeric division, such as six.

Split

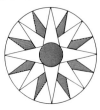

Sunburst

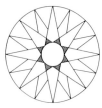

Sunflower

Concentric circle

Part One: General Principles

Mariner's Compass from New Jersey, second quarter 19th century. 96" × 93". Collection of Shelburne Museum, Vermont. Previously published in *Quilts at the Shelburne Museum,* by Lillian Baker Carlisle.

ROSAS-DOS-VENTOS NA CARTOGRAFIA PORTUGUESA ANTIGA
WIND ROSES IN EARLY PORTUGUESE CARTOGRAPHY

Wind Roses from early Portuguese cartography. A fleur-de-lis is traditionally used to indicate north. This is probably a stylization of the actual needle on the magnetic compass. The eastern point is often indicated with a cross. (*Portugoliae Monumenta Cartographica*, Armando Cortesado, Lisbon, 1960. Geographical and Maps Division, Library of Congress.)

1.
Mariner's Compass Quilts: Old and New

Detail from friendship quilt made for Mary Hudson, 1986.

The Mariner's Compass design is basically a circle. This chapter presents some ways that quiltmakers from yesterday and today have put those circles together to make wonderful quilts. There are really only a few basic ways to join quilt blocks together to make a top, but quiltmakers bring their own style to the work and the combinations create amazingly different looking quilts.

The simplest way to put the Mariner's Compass designs together is to set the circles into blocks and join them next to one another (Figure 1.1). The friendship quilt made for Mary Hudson (Color Plate 11) has a large-scale patterned fabric around the Mariner's Compass and is a good example of the "cameo" effect created when the background fabric is different from the piecing wedge.

Both Linda Otto Lipsett's and Mary Hudson's quilts were organized as friendship quilts. In her book, *Remember Me: Women and Their Friendship Quilts*, Linda tells of the fad for friendship quilts that started in the middle of the 19th century. Friendship quilts are again gaining popularity, but both the older and newer designs are usually composed of simple blocks. It is unusual to find these quilts made with Mariner's Compass designs.

Figure 1.1.
Detail of a signed friendship quilt, 1853. Collection of Linda Otto Lipsett. Previously published in *Remember Me: Women and Their Friendship Quilts.*

Part of my interest in the Mariner's Compass pattern comes from the first friendship quilt made for me (Color Plate 12). I was able to choose the pattern for this quilt and while some of my friends were at first a little intimidated by the design, everyone did a beautiful job.

Secondary designs can be created when a small appliqué design is worked in the corners of each block, as shown in Figure 1.2. A contemporary quilt with an unusual secondary design that gives an overall rippling design was made by Jane Blair in 1983 (Color Plate 3). She has chosen to use an oval Mariner's Compass, a shape that is much harder to construct than a round one because the piecing wedges that hold the design together are several different shapes instead of a single shape. Figures 1.3 and 1.4 illustrate how the circles can be economically pieced with three- or four-sided piecing units.

Figure 1.2.
Quilt from the collection of Mrs. Stanley Earl, Wells Bridge, New York. 1845-1855. 99″ × 93″. American Hurrah Antiques, New York. Previously published in the *Quilt Engagement Calendar 1984.* Cyril I. Nelson, E. P. Dutton Inc.

Separating the blocks with sashing offers many possibilities. A simple sashing is shown in my friendship quilt (Color Plate 12). Notice that the blocks are rectangular rather than square and the horizontal sashing is wider than the vertical. This quilt was designed to fit a double bed which is rectangular rather than square without adding an extra row of blocks at the bottom.

Dividing the sashing into four stripes and putting a small design in the corner of the sashing complements the already lively Mariner's Compass design in Figure 1.5. The dark background causes the Mariner's Compass to sparkle. Setting the blocks on point and adding a flying geese sashing is another exciting possibility. See Figure 1.6 for an example.

Figure 1.5. Quilt, circa 1860. 94″ × 94″. American Hurrah Antiques, New York. Previously published in the *Quilt Engagement Calendar 1985*, Cyril I. Nelson, E. P. Dutton, Inc.

Figure 1.6. Design inspired by a quilt made by Emily Gordon Chapin of Springfield, Maine, about 1840. Sturbridge Village.

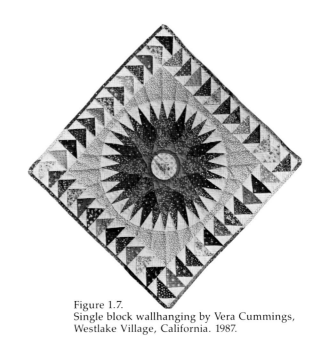

Figure 1.7.
Single block wallhanging by Vera Cummings, Westlake Village, California. 1987.

Adding an alternate block is a common arrangement. The extra space can be used to add fancy quilting as seen in Mary Strickler's beautiful quilt (Figure 1.8), which actually has a diagonal set similar to the one in Figure 1.6.

Notice how many of the quilts shown here have fancy curvilinear borders. The strong geometrics of the Mariner's Compass design are often contrasted with softer appliqué shapes.

A medallion quilt has a center design surrounded by several borders. It was a very early style of quilt commonly seen in the late 17th and early 18th century. The Mariner's Compass design is so dramatic that it is often seen in medallions. Jinny Beyer made the beautiful medallion quilt, Ray of Light, in 1977 (Figure 1.9). Her book, *Medallion Quilts*, shows several contemporary quilts with a Mariner's Compass in the center.

Figure 1.8. Quilt made by Mary R. Strickler. 1834. Bucks County, Pennsylvania. Collection of Julie Silber and Linda Reuther.

Figure 1.9. Ray of Light. Jenny Beyer. 1977. 84" × 94".

Jinny Beyer's work has inspired many medallion quilts during the current quilt revival, including my own Mariner's Medallion made in 1979. One of the borders is the traditional quilt pattern called Ocean Wave (Color Plate 2).

Another of my quilts, Wind Roses (Color Plate 4), can be thought of as a medallion with the oval in the center and a border of Mariner's Compasses around it. The arrangement was inspired partly by the page of Wind Roses shown in the Introduction and partly by the quilt in Figure 1.10 in which the compass designs are appliquéd instead of pieced.

Very small quilts are quite popular with quiltmakers now as their collection of bed quilts grows and their passion continues. I have seen a number of six-inch blocks and some four-inch blocks. Brenda Glyn-Williams has created a lovely wallhanging called Celestial Navigation in which she has combined six-inch Mariner's Compass designs with the equally complex feathered star (Color Plate 18).

The Mariner's Compass design is usually placed symmetrically in quilts either as groups or as a single central design. On maps, however, the Mariner's Compass is usually off to one side or set in "empty" space such as a body of water. My small Compass in a

Storm (Back Cover) is an example of a single Mariner's Compass offset as in a map, in a traditional Storm at Sea quilt. The bedquilt in Figure 1.11 shows the Mariner's Compass in another part of the Storm at Sea arrangement.

Figure 1.10.
From the collection of the late Edwin Binney 3rd and Gail Binney-Winslow. Circa 1840-1860. 77" × 94". Previously published in *Homage to Amanda*.

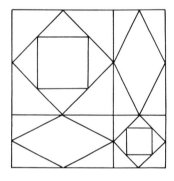

Figure 1.11.
Storm at Sea with compass. 56" × 68". Vera Cummings, Westlake Village, California. 1984.

Figure 1.12. Storm at Sea Block. See the Bibliography for information on obtaining Storm at Sea quilt patterns.

A map of the Reno–Lake Tahoe area inspired me to create the quilt called Los Angeles and Vicinity (Color Plate 7). The compass is positioned in the ocean area so that it would be on the end corner of the bed. If you are interested in making a map-style quilt, read *America's Pictorial Quilts* by Caron Mosey, in which the process of making Los Angeles and Vicinity is described.

I hope seeing these quilts has inspired you to want to make a Mariner's Compass quilt of your own design. You can create a design of your own by combining elements of one quilt with another as I did with Nautical Stars (Front Cover and Color Plate 1). The basic design comes from a Compass Rose watercolor done by an anonymous sailor during the 19th century. The other designs are from compass roses, hex signs, and antique quilts that have caught my attention during the past seven years. The small wallhanging, Fireworks (Color Plate 8), is much simpler and could feature any combination of patterns, up to 16", shown in this book.

There are 16 different Mariner's Compass patterns of various sizes in the pattern section in Part Two. Any one of these designs will fit nicely in a hoop, pillow, or other small project as well as in a full-size quilt. If none of them fits your needs, go to Chapter 3 for information about drafting your own pattern.

2.
Fabric Selection

Compass Rose from Wind Roses quilt.

When selecting fabrics for any quilt, I recommend medium-weight 100% cottons because they are easier to use. Cotton will ease and shrink better than polyester blends. Whatever the fiber content of the fabric, you should select similar weights. Try to avoid fabrics that are very slippery or too loosely woven. Cottons should be pre-shrunk and checked for bleeding. The warm colors (red, rust, maroon, etc.) seem to bleed most often. You can check for excess bleeding by wetting a small sample of fabric and laying it to dry on a white paper towel. If it leaves a colored residue, wash it again. If it still bleeds, switch to another fabric.

Contrast or value difference (amount of light and dark) is probably more important to a design than the color. We tend to respond emotionally to color. One person says, "I hate that quilt because it's purple" while another person says, "I love that quilt because it's purple." We all tend to choose colors that are our favorites, but if the design itself doesn't have enough contrast, it tends to fade into the background (Figure 2.1). So select your fabrics with attention to light, dark, and medium values (Figure 2.2). You can determine whether fabrics have contrast by laying them across one another and then squinting your eyes. If they are the same value, the line between them disappears and they blend together.

Figure 2.1.
Poor contrast

Figure 2.2.
Good contrast

Plan the background fabric of the design first. Since these Mariner's Compass designs are all pieced with pie-shaped wedges that change position around the circle, the background should be a fabric that has no obvious direction. Avoid stripes or prints that are one way or have a detectable direction; avoid solid fabrics that have very obvious grain (Figure 2.3). Closely woven solids or small overall prints are the best choice.

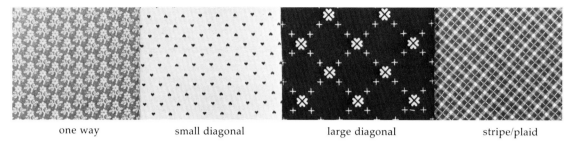

| one way | small diagonal | large diagonal | stripe/plaid |

Figure 2.3. Unsuitable background choices

Quiltmakers tend to select backgrounds from light fabrics, but Mariner's Compass designs look very dramatic on medium or dark backgrounds (Figure 2.4).

You can make the designs appear to have layers of points at different depths by selecting different graduating values for each size points. For example, use your darkest fabric for the smallest points, grading to the lightest fabric for the largest points (Figure 2.5). This also works in reverse.

Figure 2.4.
Medium
background

Figure 2.5.
Grading
values

Quilts that have prints with several different scales (size of figure) are usually more interesting than those with all the same scale prints. Larger scale prints can be used most successfully in the larger points (Figure 2.6), or positioned carefully in the centers (Figure 2.7). Stripes can be used in the points vertically or horizontally (Figure 2.6) or diagonally (Figure 2.7).

Figure 2.6   Figure 2.7

Since Mariner's Compass designs are so symmetrical, there's a tendency to use the fabric the same way in all the points, but there's no reason why each of the points couldn't be a different color. See especially Figure 2.8, and also Esther Barnwell's appliqué medallion in Color Plate 17. The 12-point designs lend themselves particularly well to rainbow colors, as seen in Fireworks (Color Plates 8 and 9).

Concentric circle variations can appear to be see-through if you make the base of the points from fabric similar to the background (Figure 2.7). Or make those same pieces from a contrasting fabric and you'll see what appears to be a ring or plate behind or between the layers of points (Figure 2.9).

Figure 2.8.
Detail from
Nautical Stars quilt

Figure 2.9.
Detail from
Wind Roses quilt

One more word about the background: there is really no reason why it has to remain the same throughout the design. It could change value around the circle. This can be a real challenge since that means all the points have to change value as well as continue to have contrast, but it can be spectacular, as seen in Nautical Stars in Figure 2.10 and on the front cover.

An interesting variation seen on many map compasses is known as shadowing. When the points are split they are normally arranged symmetrically with the light and dark on the same sides around the circle (Figure 2.9). To shadow a Mariner's Compass, imagine a light source on one side illuminating the points so both sides of adjacent points are light. As the points move around the compass, they meet with two dark sides adjacent on the opposite sides (Figure 2.11).

Figure 2.10.
Detail from
Nautical Stars quilt

Figure 2.11.
Detail from
Wind Roses quilt

To make a shadowed Mariner's Compass, cut half of the split points with light on the right side and half with the light on the left side. If you sew the two fabrics together before cutting, just cut half with the template pointing one direction and half pointing the other direction (Figure 2.12).

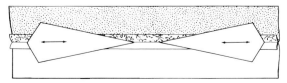

Figure 2.12

3.
Drafting

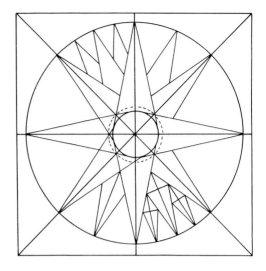

Quiltmakers are frequently wary of drafting their own patterns. However, unless your quilt book library includes all the books and patterns published, there will probably come a day when you will want a special pattern in a specific size. It makes me feel extremely creative to draft my own patterns and it sometimes is less work than combing through the books and patterns to find just the right one. Drafting is often the only way to make a pattern fit.

SUPPLIES AND TOOLS

— *Graph paper.* ¼″ or ⅛″ grid. Use the 8½″ × 11″ size for the 6″ practice exercises; 17″ × 22″ is available for larger designs.
— *Adjustable drafting compass.* A compass that spreads to at least 6″ is best; one with a fixed arm helps maintain accuracy. An extension arm is helpful, but you can also use a ruler with holes to make the larger circles, as illustrated in Figure 3.2. If you need a larger circle, get a yardstick or beam compass from an art supply store.
— *18″ clear plastic ruler with holes.*
— *Sharp pencils and eraser.* Mechanical pencils in sizes 0.5mm or 0.7mm are excellent.
— *Protractor.* You'll need this for divisions other than eight.

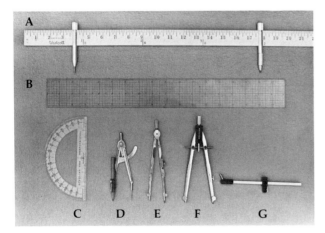

Figure 3.1.
A. Yardstick compass
B. Plastic ruler
C. Protractor
D. Friction compass
E. Compass from drafting set
F. Fixed compass
G. Extension

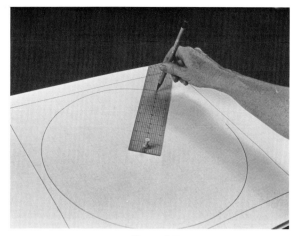

Figure 3.2

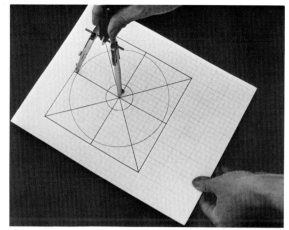

Figure 3.3

DRAFTING EXERCISE

The following exercise should be done with a 6″ square practice size. Once you know how to draft a basic Mariner's Compass, you can then draft your own variation in the size you require. Work with graph paper on a pad of paper (so that the drafting compass point doesn't move) and keep your pencils sharp.

1. Draw a 6″ square with horizontal and vertical lines in the middle (Figure 3.3).
2. Draw a 1½″ circle in the middle of the square (¾″ radius). This is the drafting circle and will be used to determine the width of the points (Figure 3.3). If you would like the points to be fatter, use a larger circle. A smaller circle results in thinner points.
3. Set the drafting compass point in the center and the pencil/marker arm ¼″ in from the top of the square. Swing the compass to make the outer circle (Figure 3.3). (The background is easier to piece if the Mariner's Compass is set at least ¼″ inside the square.)
4. Hold the drafting compass by the top, not the side arm. If you have trouble swinging the compass accurately, try holding it firmly and turning the paper under it (Figure 3.3).
5. Starting at the top (north) of the outer circle, place the ruler along the edge of the drafting circle and draw a line from point A to point B (Figure 3.4). Repeat on the other side of the drafting circle. Continue with the bottom of the vertical line and both sides of the horizontal line. You should now have the four-pointed design as seen in Figure 3.5.

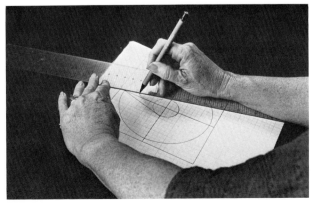

Figure 3.4

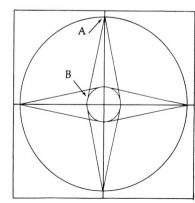

Figure 3.5

6. Draw diagonal lines from each corner of the square to the center and then, using the ruler, draw a line from C to D (Figure 3.6). Continue drawing lines using the drafting circle and diagonals to complete the next four points (Figure 3.7).

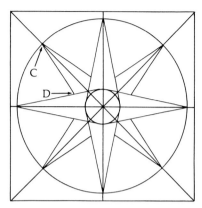

Figure 3.6   Figure 3.7

7. Find the position for the sixteenth point by setting the drafting compass as wide as the distance between the points (Figure 3.8). Swing the drafting compass from point E out into the area of the paper beyond the square and mark an arc (Figure 3.9). Move the point of the drafting compass so that the point swings from F and mark a crossing arc (see Figure 3.9 and 3.10) at point G. Place a ruler along the line from the center point and the crossing of the arcs and mark a new sixteenth-point position on the large circle. This procedure is called bisecting. You can use this method to accurately divide any curved space in half. Use the drafting circle to draw the sides of the new Mariner's Compass points. See Figure 3.10.

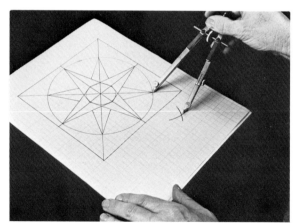

Figure 3.8   Figure 3.9

8. Mariner's Compass designs often have 32 points. To find a thirty-second-point position, bisect the new wedge (Figure 3.11). Use the drafting circle to draw the sides of the new point. Most Mariner's Compass designs on quilts stop at 32 points, like the compass card, but occasionally you do find 64 points like the marvelous quilt from the Shelburne Museum shown at the beginning of Part One. To draft a 64-point Mariner's Compass, bisect the new wedge and make a new set of points to get 64. Be sure to make your center drafting circle relatively small because it leaves more space in the outside wedges for the points.

9. At this stage in the drafting, you have all the pattern shapes necessary to make a 16- or 32-point Split Mariner's Compass (Figure 3.12). It is not necessary to draft the complete design in order to have the pattern shapes necessary for the templates. However, it is helpful to have a complete design to help you visualize fabric placement and the piecing sequence.

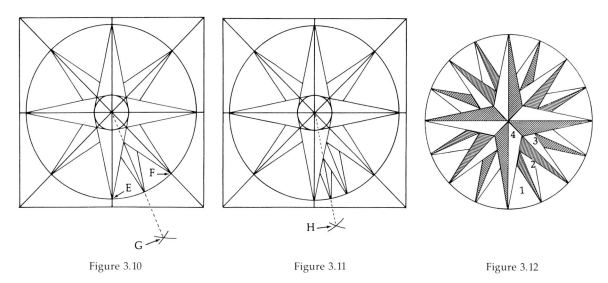

Figure 3.10   Figure 3.11   Figure 3.12

VARIATIONS

The *Sunburst variation* has a circle in the center and the points are usually not split. To create the appliqué center for the Sunburst Mariner's Compass, set the drafting compass point in the center and the pencil point on the intersection of the sides of the north and west points (point I in Figure 3.13) and draw a new, larger circle.

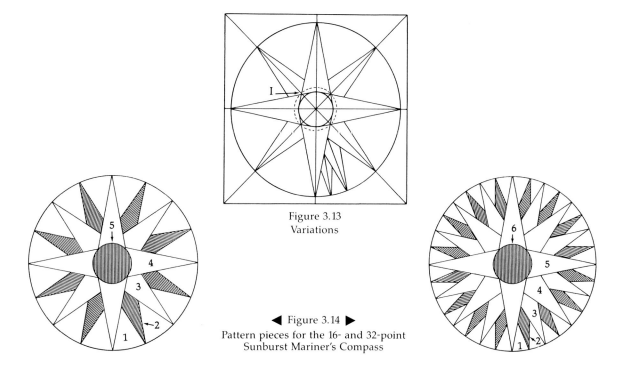

Figure 3.13
Variations

◀ Figure 3.14 ▶
Pattern pieces for the 16- and 32-point
Sunburst Mariner's Compass

The *Sunflower variation* of Mariner's Compass has an inner circle of points around the center. Extend the side of the diagonal points from J to K (Figure 3.15). See Figure 2.10 for a photograph of a Sunflower variation.

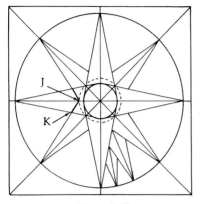

Figure 3.15

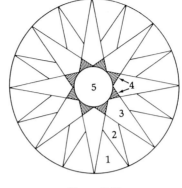

Figure 3.16

Pattern pieces for the Sunflower Mariner's Compass

For a *Concentric Circle variation,* the base of the points can be divided horizontally. Set the drafting compass point in the center and extend the pencil/marker arm to where the sixteenth point intersects the sides of the adjoining points. Draw a curve across the top of each sixteenth point, skipping all the others (Figure 3.17). Concentric circles can be drawn on any point. You can make the design easier to piece if you use a straight line instead of a curved line (Figure 3.17). See Figure 2.11 for a photograph of a concentric circle variation.

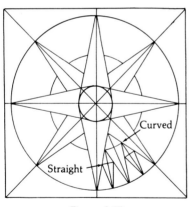

Figure 3.17

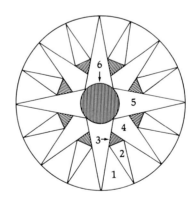

Figure 3.18

Pattern pieces for the Concentric Circle Mariner's Compass

Some compass rose designs from maps have different width points within the same design although most quilt designs do not. Figure 3.19 illustrates a variety of point widths. If you wish to make some points fat and some thin, then vary the size of the drafting circle. Different width points make the design more interesting, but they also create asymmetrical piecing wedges. The piecing wedges on the right and left sides of the points will have to be marked and cut by flipping the template over (Figure 3.20). See Figure 2.9 for a photograph of an example.

Another interesting variation has the points at different depths within the design. A new outer ring is created and the ends of the points touch this new circle (Figure 3.21). See Figure 2.9 for a photograph of an example.

Figure 3.19

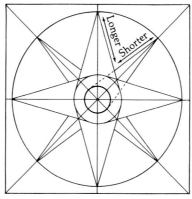

Figure 3.20

Figure 3.21

Other Star Designs

What I call *Other Star designs*—those that look like Mariner's Compass but are not divisible by eight—are frequently used in quilt designs. Examples of these shown in the pattern section are Hexagonal Star with 12 points, Rainbow Star with 24 points, Pentagon Star with 20 points, and Twilight Star with 20 points.

1. The easiest way to draft these designs is to use a protractor to find the points on a circle. Divide the number of desired points into 360 degrees to find the number of degrees separating the points.

> *To get 6 points:*
> — 360 divided by 6 equals 60
> — mark every 60 degrees
> (60, 120, 180, 240, 300, 360)
>
> *To get 5 points:*
> — 360 divided by 5 equals 72
> — mark every 72 degrees
> (72, 144, 216, 288, 360)
>
> *To get 9 points:*
> — 360 divided by 9 equals 40
> — mark every 40 degrees
> (40, 80, 120, 160, 200, 240, 280, 320, 360)

2. Draw a square and circle with a center point and a vertical line extending to the top. Align the protractor with 0 at the top on the vertical line and mark off the desired points (Figure 3.22). To mark points after 180, reverse the protractor (Figure 3.23) and use 180 less, i.e., for 216 use 36 (216−180=36).
3. Use a ruler to line up the desired points with the center dot. Select a drafting circle (larger diameter for fat points, smaller diameter for thin points) and draw in the sides of the points (see Figure 3.24 for an example with six points). These designs can have all the variations, i.e., split, sunburst, etc., that the regular Mariner's Compass has. You can divide the spaces between the points by bisecting the wedge.

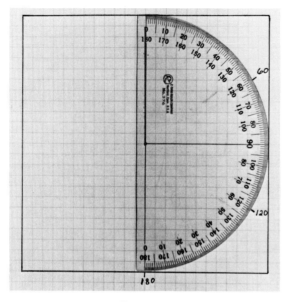

Figure 3.22

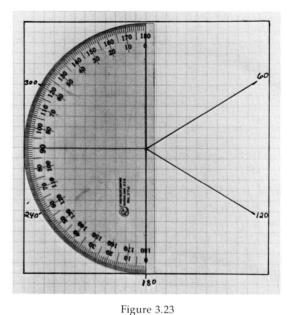

Figure 3.23

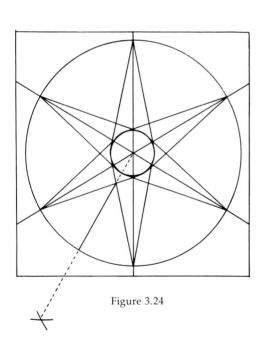

Figure 3.24

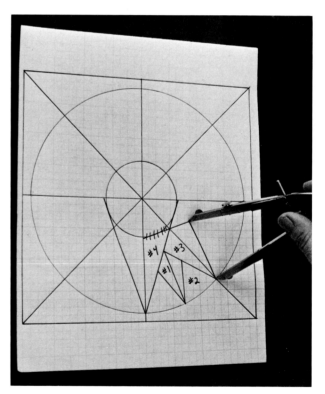

Figure 3.25

Once you have mastered the techniques for drafting these designs, you should draft your chosen design in the desired size. By drafting your own pattern and combining these variations, you can create a unique Mariner's Compass design.

Make a full-size drawing of the design with all of the pieces that will be necessary to make the templates. Use the drafting compass to check the lengths of both sides of a point or piecing wedge to make sure they are accurate (Figure 3.25). See Chapter 2 for advice on fabric selection.

4.
Construction

Detail from Wind Roses quilt.

The Mariner's Compass block in Figure 4.1 is from a well-used antique quilt in my collection. The construction techniques are not very precise. Not only are the points wobbly and the concentric circles scalloped instead of round, but the points range from blunt to very blunt and occasionally do not come near the circle at all. All nine blocks show the same level of skill. It could have been pieced by a child or person with poor vision, but in spite of the workmanship it still has great graphic appeal (Back Cover). To avoid wobbly seams and blunt points, try to maintain a reasonable level of accuracy during the whole process, starting with drafting, making templates, marking and cutting the fabric, as well as with the sewing.

MAKING TEMPLATES

Whether you draft your own patterns or use the ones in this book, great care should be taken to insure accuracy at all times.

The patterns show a sewing line and a cutting line with a ¼" seam allowance except for the appliqué patterns, which show only the sewing line. If you are sewing by hand, make a template from the pattern with the sewing line. If you plan to use the sewing machine, make a template from the pattern with the cutting line.

Figure 4.1

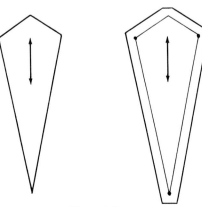

Figure 4.2

Make a set of templates by carefully tracing each pattern piece onto tracing paper. Be sure to include all the information such as name of pattern, letter, number of pieces to be cut, grainline, and any matching marks. The "R" in the cutting notation means reverse. Cut the number advised and then flip the pattern piece face down and cut the remaining number.

Cut roughly around the pattern piece (outside the cutting line). Glue each piece to lightweight cardboard or plastic. Cut through both pieces precisely on the line for each pattern piece.

You may be tempted to use a photocopy machine to reproduce the patterns instead of tracing them. Please be aware that nearly all photocopy processes enlarge by at least 1% or 2%, but worse than that, they sometimes enlarge in one direction and not in the other.

The patterns for the split point variations have been given as a whole point except for Patterns 1 and 3. Sew two strips of contrasting fabrics together and then center the whole point and mark as illustrated in Figure 4.3.

Fabric that is printed or woven with stripes of contrasting values can be used for the split points instead of sewing two fabrics together (Figure 4.4). This saves sewing time and eliminates the bulk of seams at the ends of the points.

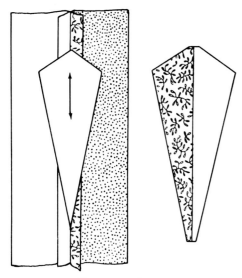

Figure 4.3. Sewn stripe

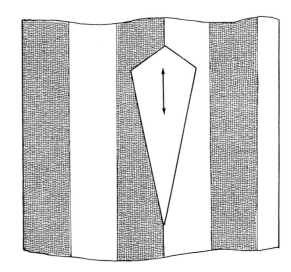

Figure 4.4. Printed stripe

MARKING FABRIC

Place the template on the back of the fabric with the printing up. It is very important that all the marking be done very precisely. When marking around the hand-sewing template, first mark at the point of each angle of the template and then draw lines between them (Figure 4.5).

If you are using the hand-sewing template with only the sewing line, you will have to add a seam allowance on the fabric by marking ¼" with a ruler (Figure 4.5) or by simply estimating that amount. The machine-sewing template has a ¼" seam allowance included.

You will need to use a ¼″ gauge on your sewing machine throat plate or use the edge of the presser foot, if it is ¼″. You can mark the throat plate yourself with tape. I find it's very helpful when machine piecing to also mark dots on the fabric at the intersections of the sewing line. These dots can be made by punching a hole through the template with a small hole punch or with a sharp pointed instrument, such as the end of the drafting compass, and then using a pencil to mark the fabric through the hole (Figure 4.6). When preparing to sew the pieces by machine, line up these dots and pin them together, then sew carefully through the dots.

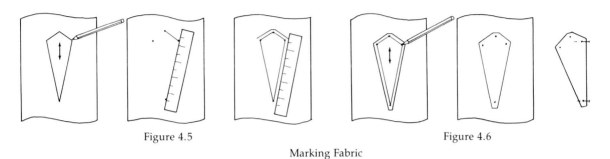

Figure 4.5   Figure 4.6

Marking Fabric

GENERAL PIECING SEQUENCE

All compass designs are pieced similarly with slight differences according to design variation. Starting from the outside, the smallest points are pieced between background wedges to form a new larger wedge (Figure 4.7). The process is continued with the new wedge being joined to the next size point and continued until all the background wedges and points are assembled.

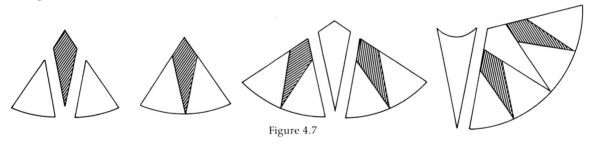

Figure 4.7

Sunburst variation can be pieced into asymmetrical quarters and the centers can be appliquéd last.

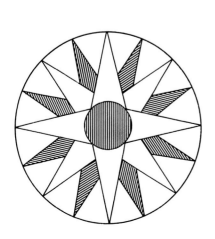

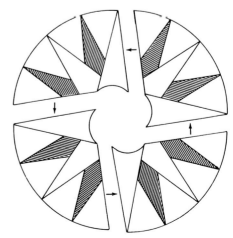

Figure 4.8
Sunburst

Split Point variations are of two types. If the center is joined with a circle as in Figure 2.9, then the splits should all be sewn together first and then continue with piecing as shown in Figure 4.7. They can be cut from pre-sewn fabric (Figure 4.3) or from wide stripe printed fabric (Figure 4.4).

If the design meets in the center with eight seams as in Figure 2.4, then they can be constructed into eighths, making it easier to piece. Sew only the smallest split points together and then assemble as illustrated in Figure 4.9.

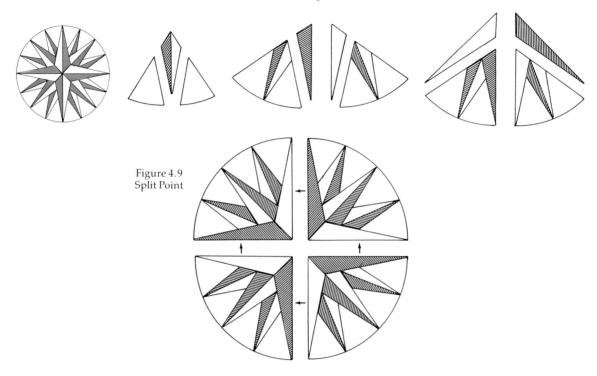

Figure 4.9
Split Point

All of the patterns in this book show the template as one piece except for Patterns 1 and 3. If you are drafting your own patterns, you will need to make two templates (one for the dark and one for the light) and add seam allowance all the way around each piece.

For the ***Sunflower variation,*** the small triangles in the center are pieced to the base of the largest points, as in Figure 4.10; then continue as illustrated.

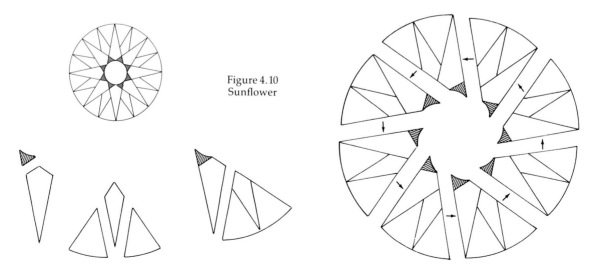

Figure 4.10
Sunflower

With the *Concentric Circle variation,* the triangles at the base of the points are pieced on first to complete the point, as in Figure 4.11. Then continue the piecing sequence as illustrated.

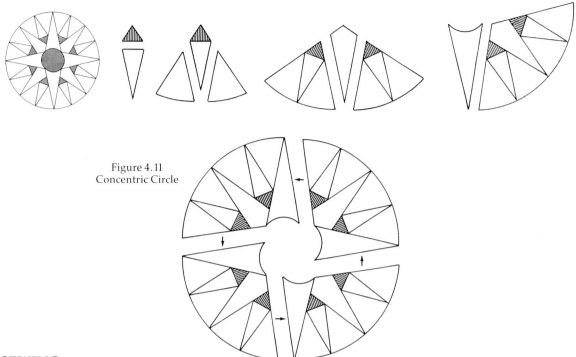

Figure 4.11
Concentric Circle

SEWING

Keep in mind that the sides of the points are on the bias and can easily stretch—so handle them carefully. Pin at the intersections and ease if the fabric has stretched. If you are hand-piecing, sew with small even stitches approximately 10 to 12 to the inch. There should be a ¼″ seam allowance at the tip of the point after it is stitched (Figure 4.12).

If you are hand-piecing, be sure to close up the seam at the tip of the point. If you are sewing on the machine, the seam allowances at the intersections will be stitched all the way through. This keeps the tips of the points sharp when the circles are joined to the background.

All seam allowances should be pressed away from the points at the outside of the completed circle (Figure 4.12). The bulk from the seam allowances is more easily controlled this way.

Figure 4.12

The center circles in the designs can be pieced, but I prefer to appliqué them on. Prepare a paper template the finished size of the circle. Baste the fabric to the paper (Figure 4.13). This will insure that the circle stays round. Appliqué the circle into position with small stitches. Remove the top basting, cut away the back fabric if necessary, and remove the paper. I make paper template circles for the small central pieced stars as well (Patterns 5, 7, 8, and 9). After the central star is pieced, baste it to a paper template. Appliqué it to the larger center circle (if given) and cut the backing fabric away later. The center circle can be appliquéd before or after the Mariner's Compass is blocked.

BLOCKING

After the Mariner's Compass is pieced into a circle, it should be blocked to insure accuracy. Draw a circle the size of the finished design on a piece of fabric or paper; place it on your ironing board or other surface to which it can be pinned. Mark the center, top, and sides. Gently ease the compass block into this shape by pinning opposing points, one set at a time. Press with a steam iron and allow the fabric to cool, or spray with a fine spray and let it air dry. Remove the pins, turn the block over, and press it lightly to encourage the seams to lie flat (Figure 4.14).

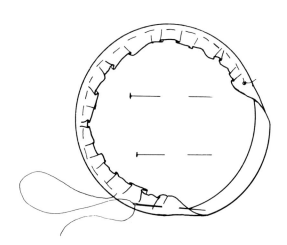

Figure 4.13

Figure 4.14

ATTACHING TO BACKGROUND

The easiest way to get the pieced Mariner's Compass circle into a background is to have the background cut into a square and appliqué directly. This method does waste fabric since the fabric behind the Mariner's Compass is removed later.

Appliqué

Baste the outer edge of the blocked Mariner's Compass circle back ¼". Position the circle on the background and appliqué it on with small stitches (Figure 4.15). Remove the top basting and cut the background fabric away from behind the block, leaving a ¼" seam allowance. Clip this seam and press away from the Mariner's Compass points (Figure 4.16).

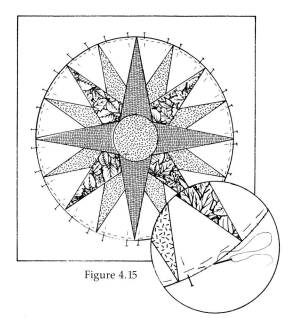

Figure 4.15

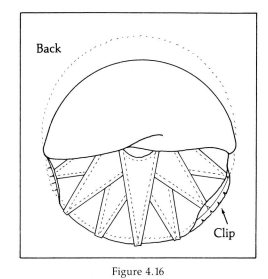

Figure 4.16

Piecing

If you prefer to piece the circle into the background, baste the seam allowance back as for appliqué. Pin to the background square and, using a blind stitch or ladder stitch (Figure 4.17), baste the circle to the background with ½″ stitches. Remove the top basting, cut the background from behind the circle, and use the blind stitch basting as a guide to piecing. Press the seam allowance away from the center. The background seam allowance may need to be clipped at the top, bottom, and sides, as in Figure 4.16.

A more fabric-efficient way to set the circle into the background is to draft the background area into four quarter-circle shapes (Figure 4.18) and piece the curved seams.

See Figures 1.3 and 1.4 for sample three- or four-sided piecing units if you wish to construct a whole top of Mariner's Compass circles set very close to one another.

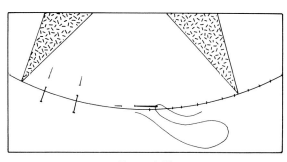

Figure 4.17

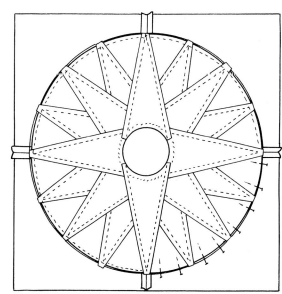

Figure 4.18

QUILTING

The Mariner's Compass design lends itself well to structural quilting, or quilting within the pieces themselves. Since the seam allowances have been pressed away from the points, it is easy to quilt inside the points, as illustrated in the center of Figure 4.19.

The angle of the smaller points on the quilt can be continued through the larger points (as seen on the left side of Figure 4.19), and new points can even be quilted in. A line can be drawn through the middle of each point and between each point (as seen on the right side of Figure 4.19).

Quilting lines that radiate from the center can be a problem in that they are closer in the middle and further apart as they go out, creating an uneven amount of quilting. A discontinuous line can be added to even the spacing (as seen on the right side of Figure 4.19).

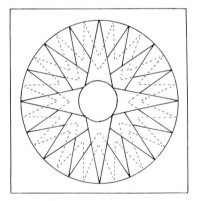 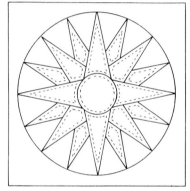 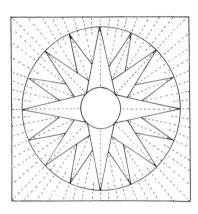

Figure 4.19

Figure 4.20.
The quilting on Wind Roses (Color Plate 4) was inspired by the lines on this navigational sea chart from the 16th century.

2. *Mariner's Medallion*
   at Bodega Head,
   California
   Judy Mathieson
   1979. 75″ × 95″

3. *Mariner's Compass*
   Jane Blair
   Conshohocken,
   Pennsylvania
   1983. 80″ × 90″

4. Wind Roses
Judy Mathieson
1983. 80" × 102"
Based on 16th-century
navigational charts.
Compass designs are
14" to 16" in diameter.

5. Wind Roses
back view

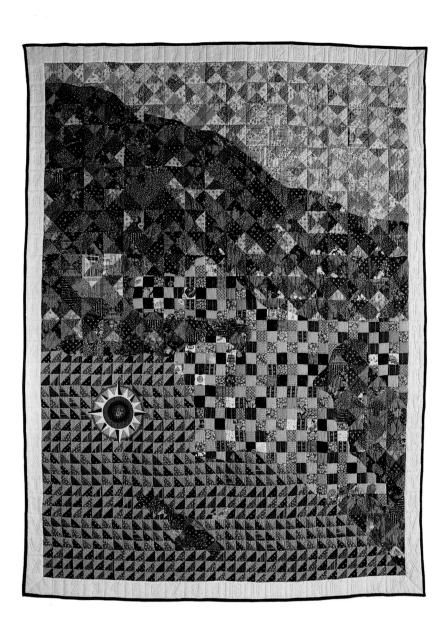

6. *Los Angeles and Vicinity*
Judy Mathieson
1982. 72″ × 96″
Map co-ordinates are quilted into the border so that "points of interest" can be located.

7. *Los Angeles and Vicinity*
detail
11″ compass diameter
The figured fabrics represent "points of interest" such as Los Angeles International Airport, Marina del Rey, La Brea Tarpits, Hollywood, Los Angeles Zoo, Disney Studios, Dodger Stadium, etc.

8. Fireworks
Judy Mathieson
1987. 36″ × 36″
Hexagonal Star, Compass and Stars, and Rainbow Star (see the Pattern section) are used in this small wallhanging.

9. Fireworks
detail of Rainbow Star
12″ diameter

10. Mauna Kea Nights
Danita Rafalovich
Los Angeles,
California
1987. 60″ × 80″
Unquilted top

11. Compass Rose
Mary Hudson and
friends
San Juan Bautista,
California
1986. 100″ × 100″
Unquilted top

**12. Sunburst Mariner's
Compass**
Judy Mathieson and
friends
1980. 85″ × 95″

**13. 16-Point Mariner's
Compass**
Maker unknown
Circa 1880. 90″ × 90″
Collection of Mary
Hudson

14. *Pentagon Star*
Fresno, California
1875. 70″ × 87″
Private collection

15. *Pentagon Star*
detail

16. *32-Point Mariner's Compass* and detail
Maker unknown
Factoryville,
Pennsylvania
Circa 1880. 80″ × 80″
Collection of Sandra
Thlick and Katalin
Stazer, Los Angeles,
California

17. Rose Compass Quilt
Esther Barnwell
Signal Mountain,
Tennessee
1981. 90″ × 98″

18. Celestial Navigation
Brenda Glyn-Williams
Woodland Hills,
California
1987. 43″ × 43″

19. Celestial Navigation
detail

Part Two: Patterns

Mariner's Medallion. Judy Mathieson. 1979. 75″ × 95″

INTRODUCTION

Take my advice and start with the simplest design if you have never worked with a Mariner's Compass before. Pattern 1 is a combination pattern that will give you several different Mariner's Compass designs with the basic variations and some combinations; the eight designs in the Combination Star are listed in the order of their complexity, starting with the simplest. Remember, a 16-point design is simpler than a 32-point design because it has half as many pieces.

See Chapter 4 for advice on how to make templates from these patterns. All of the patterns are given as circles. If you wish to make them as square blocks and do not wish to appliqué or piece them into a whole square, turn to the end of this section to find the corner pieces for Patterns 1 through 8.

Unquilted wall hanging by Judy Mathieson. 1987. 36" × 41". Includes Sunflower with Star, Pentagon Star, Hexagon Star and Twilight Star (one-quarter).

Pattern 1

COMBINATION STAR
with Variations
11″ diameter for 12″ block

The patterns given here can be combined to create the eight different designs shown. Select the design you want to make, then find the listing of the pattern pieces necessary. Cut the pattern pieces and refer to Chapter 4 for the piecing sequence.

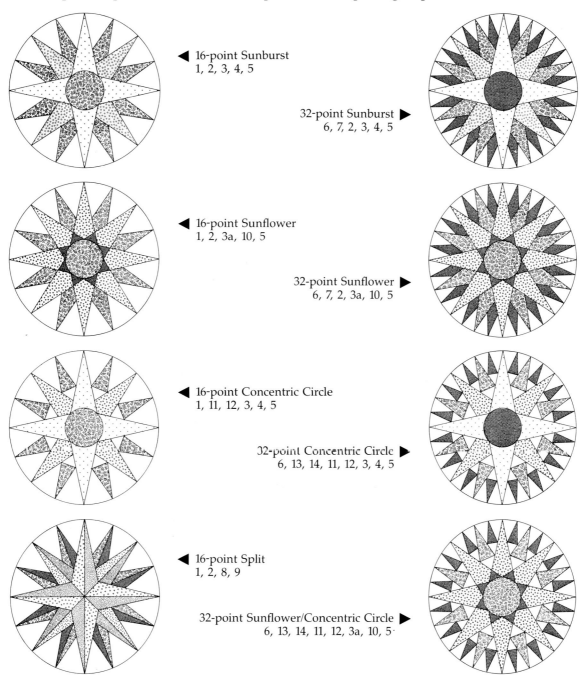

◀ 16-point Sunburst
1, 2, 3, 4, 5

32-point Sunburst ▶
6, 7, 2, 3, 4, 5

◀ 16-point Sunflower
1, 2, 3a, 10, 5

32-point Sunflower ▶
6, 7, 2, 3a, 10, 5

◀ 16-point Concentric Circle
1, 11, 12, 3, 4, 5

32-point Concentric Circle ▶
6, 13, 14, 11, 12, 3, 4, 5

◀ 16-point Split
1, 2, 8, 9

32-point Sunflower/Concentric Circle ▶
6, 13, 14, 11, 12, 3a, 10, 5

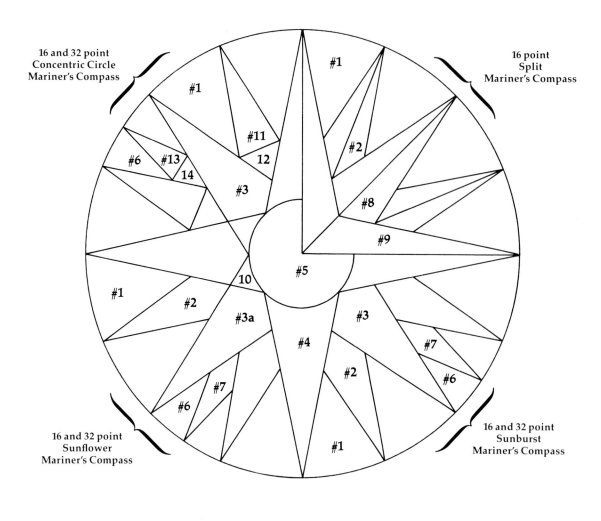

16 and 32 point
Concentric Circle
Mariner's Compass

16 point
Split
Mariner's Compass

16 and 32 point
Sunflower
Mariner's Compass

16 and 32 point
Sunburst
Mariner's Compass

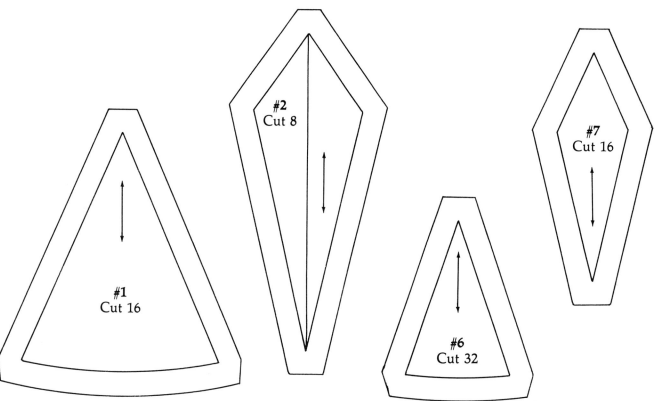

#1
Cut 16

#2
Cut 8

#6
Cut 32

#7
Cut 16

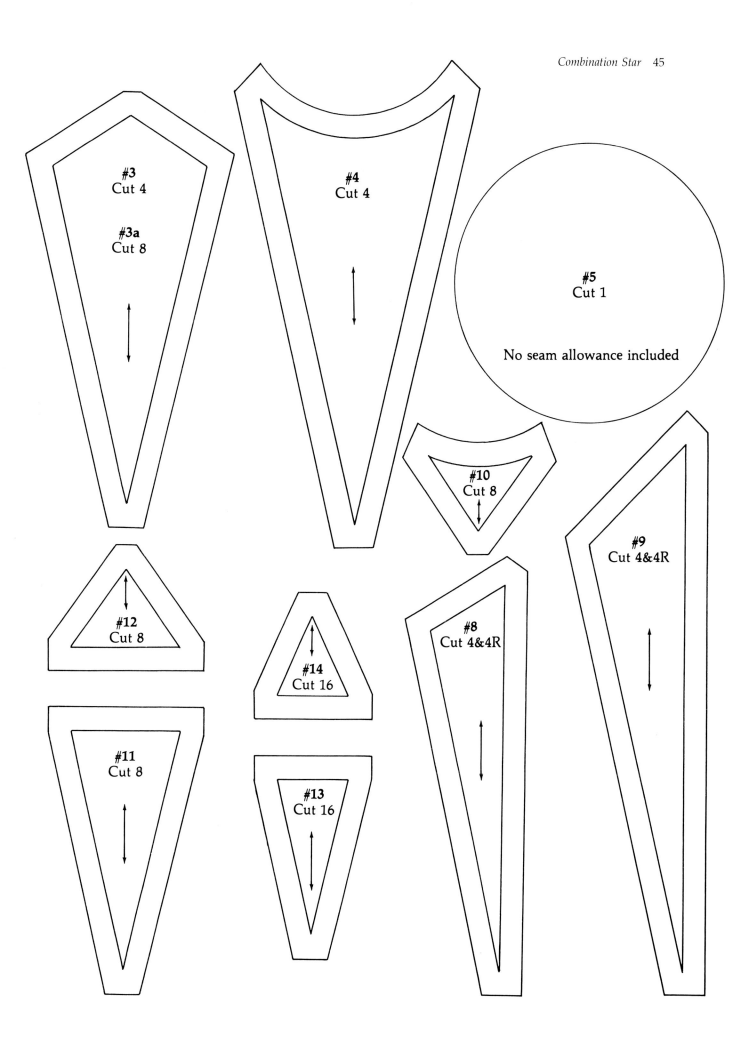

#3
Cut 4

#3a
Cut 8

#4
Cut 4

#5
Cut 1

No seam allowance included

#10
Cut 8

#9
Cut 4&4R

#12
Cut 8

#14
Cut 16

#8
Cut 4&4R

#11
Cut 8

#13
Cut 16

Pattern 2

HEXAGONAL STAR
9″ diameter for 10″ block

This is an old pattern often seen in red and white or blue and white. Be sure to use the matching marks on each side of piecing wedge #1 (as one side is longer than the other). See the general piecing instructions for the concentric circle-type Mariner's Compass. The hexagon center can be pieced-in last or appliquéd. An example of this design is in the upper left side of Nautical Stars (Color Plate 1) and in the Fireworks wallhanging (Color Plate 8).

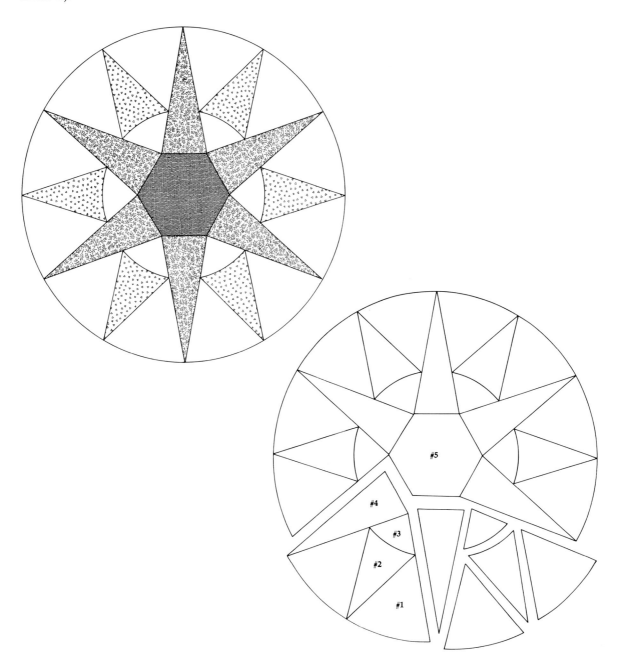

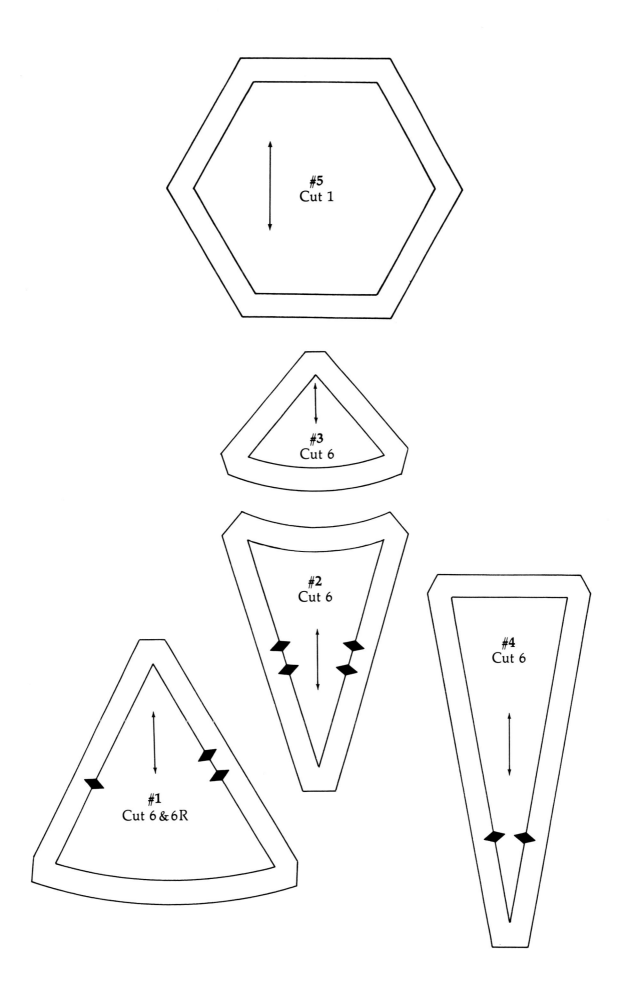

#5
Cut 1

#3
Cut 6

#2
Cut 6

#4
Cut 6

#1
Cut 6 & 6R

Pattern 3

SUNFLOWER WITH STAR
9″ diameter for 10″ block

See the general piecing instructions for the sunflower-type Mariner's Compass for the outside of this star, and for a modified version of the split Mariner's Compass for the inside star. The center star is pieced into the outside circle, or appliquéd, after both have been completed. Both the split (#5 and #6) and the whole pattern piece (#5a and #6a) are included for your convenience. An example of this design is shown in the upper right side of Nautical Stars (Color Plate 1).

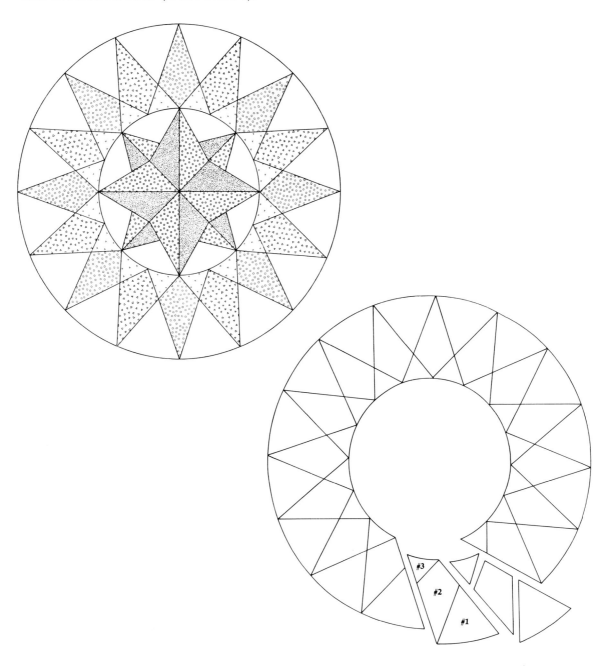

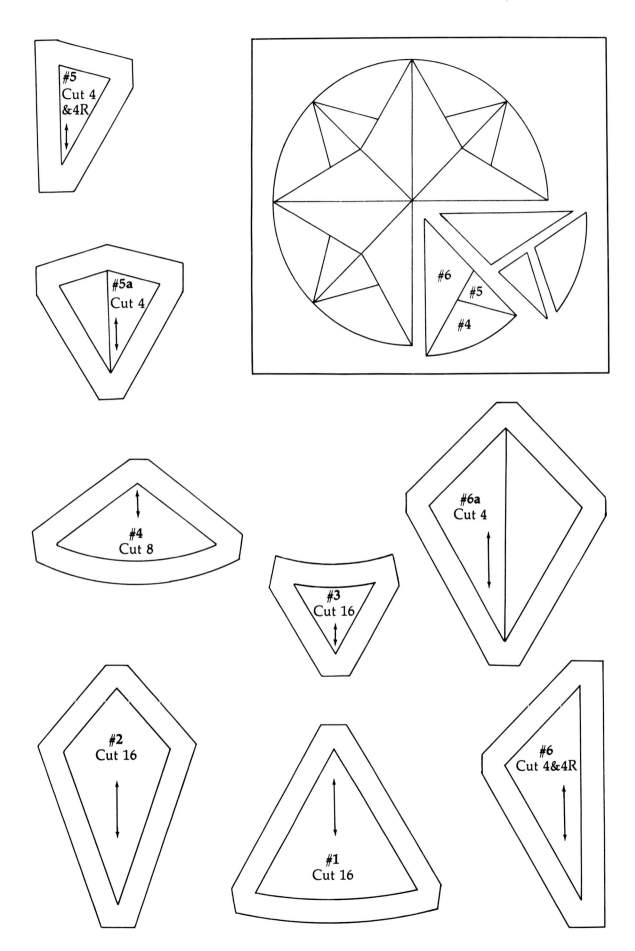

#5
Cut 4
&4R

#5a
Cut 4

#6
#5
#4

#4
Cut 8

#6a
Cut 4

#3
Cut 16

#2
Cut 16

#1
Cut 16

#6
Cut 4&4R

Pattern 4

RAINBOW STAR
10″ diameter for 12″ block

This is a very old quilt design reproduced from some circa 1830–1840 blocks in my collection. The piecing is more difficult than on most Mariner's Compass designs because of the set-in piecing at the intersection of #3, #4, and #5. More examples of this design can be seen in the upper left side of Nautical Stars (Color Plate 1) and in the Fireworks wallhanging (Color Plate 8).

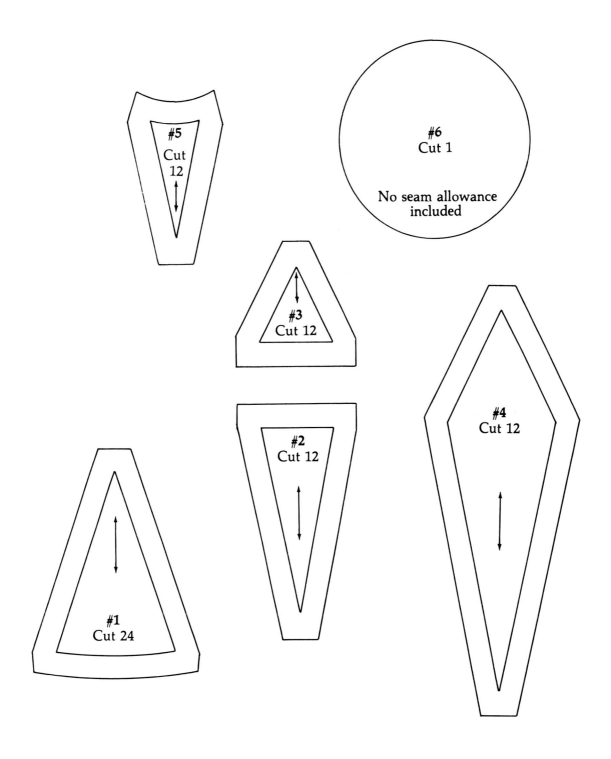

#5
Cut
12

#6
Cut 1

No seam allowance
included

#3
Cut 12

#2
Cut 12

#4
Cut 12

#1
Cut 24

Pattern 5

SAINT AUGUSTINE COMPASS
12″ diameter for 14″ block

I found this design in a newspaper in Saint Augustine, Florida. The design is shadowed, as described in Chapter 2 and as illustrated in Figure 2.11. See the general piecing instructions for the sunburst variations. The illustration indicates that the points are split, but the pattern pieces are for the full point. Pre-sew strips of fabric together and then cut as shown in Figure 2.12. Sew the small circles on the four major points after the circle is attached to the background. An example of this design is shown in the upper right side of Nautical Stars (Color Plate 1).

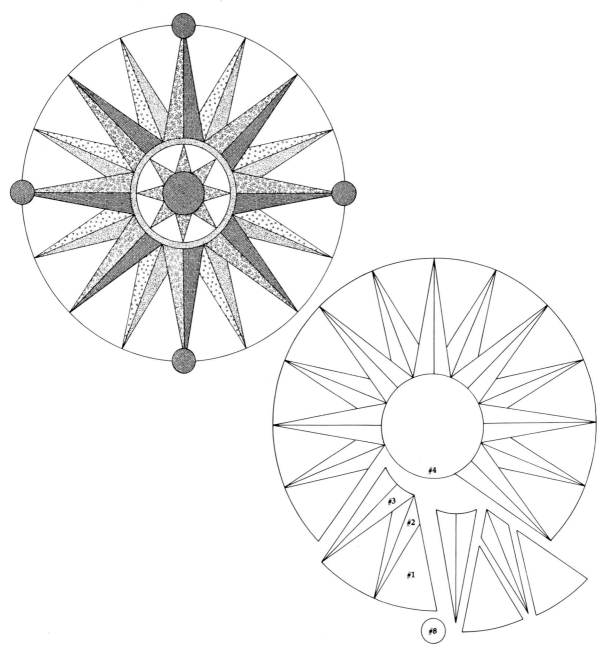

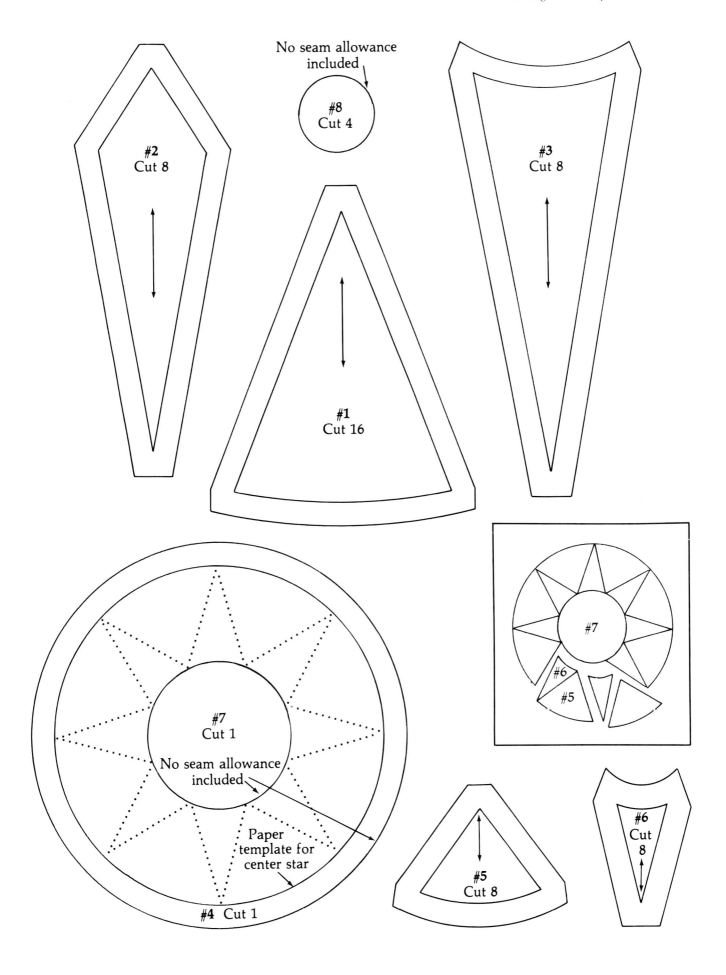

No seam allowance
included

#8
Cut 4

#2
Cut 8

#3
Cut 8

#1
Cut 16

#7
Cut 1

No seam allowance
included

Paper
template for
center star

#4 Cut 1

#7

#6

#5

#5
Cut 8

#6
Cut
8

Pattern 6

PENTAGON STAR
14″ diameter for 16″ block

The design was inspired by the antique quilt in Color Plate 15. Use the general piecing instructions for concentric circle variations. An example of this design is shown on the upper right side of Nautical Stars (Color Plate 1).

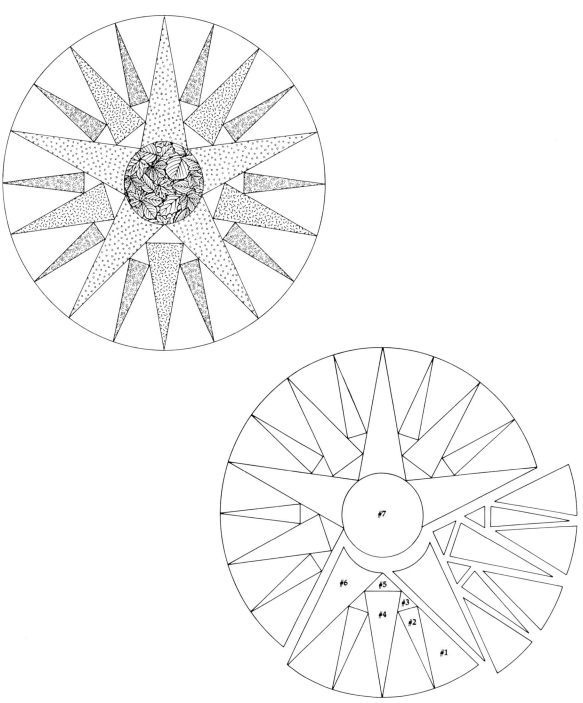

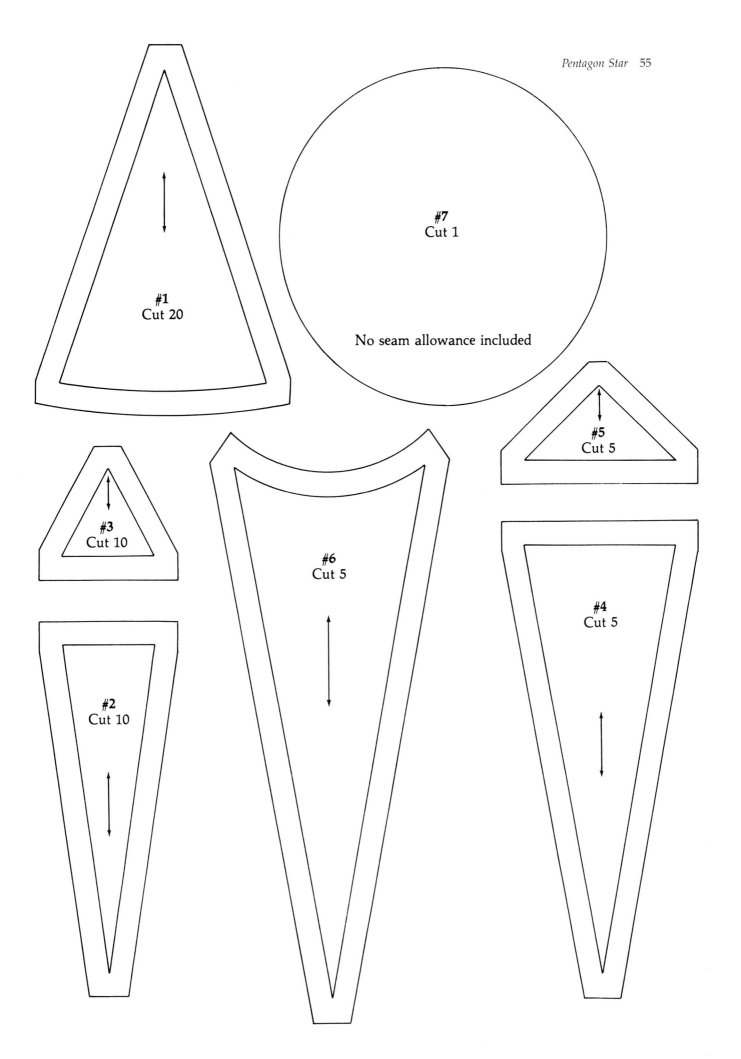

Pattern 7

COMPASS ROSE
with Fleur-de-lis
16″ diameter for 18″ block

This compass rose comes from a 15th-century map by Jan Blau. Use the general piecing instructions for concentric circle variations for the outside star; use the sunburst variation for the inside star. After the Compass Rose has been pieced, the fleur-de-lis can be appliquéd into position. An example of this design can be seen on the middle left side of Wind Roses (Color Plate 4) and Mary Hudson's Compass Rose (Color Plate 11). This design was previously published in *Lady's Circle Patchwork Quilt Magazine,* Summer 1984.

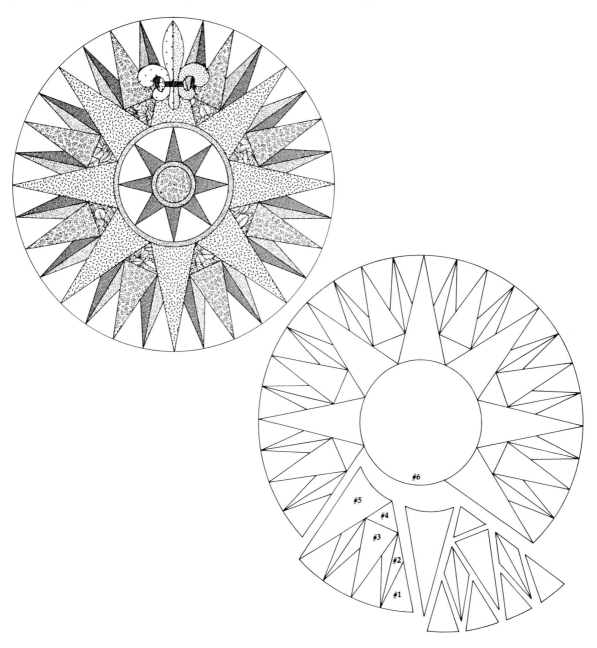

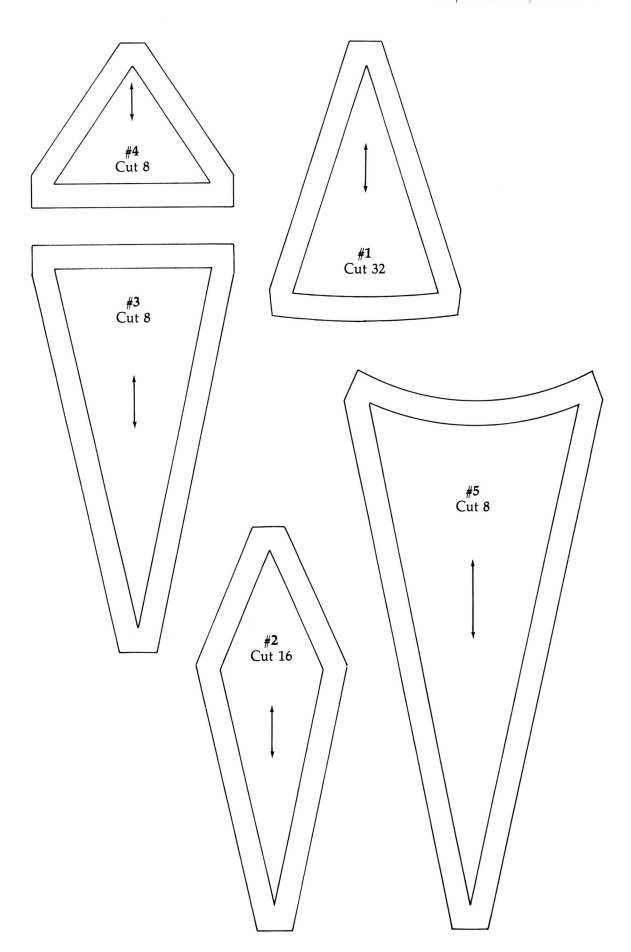

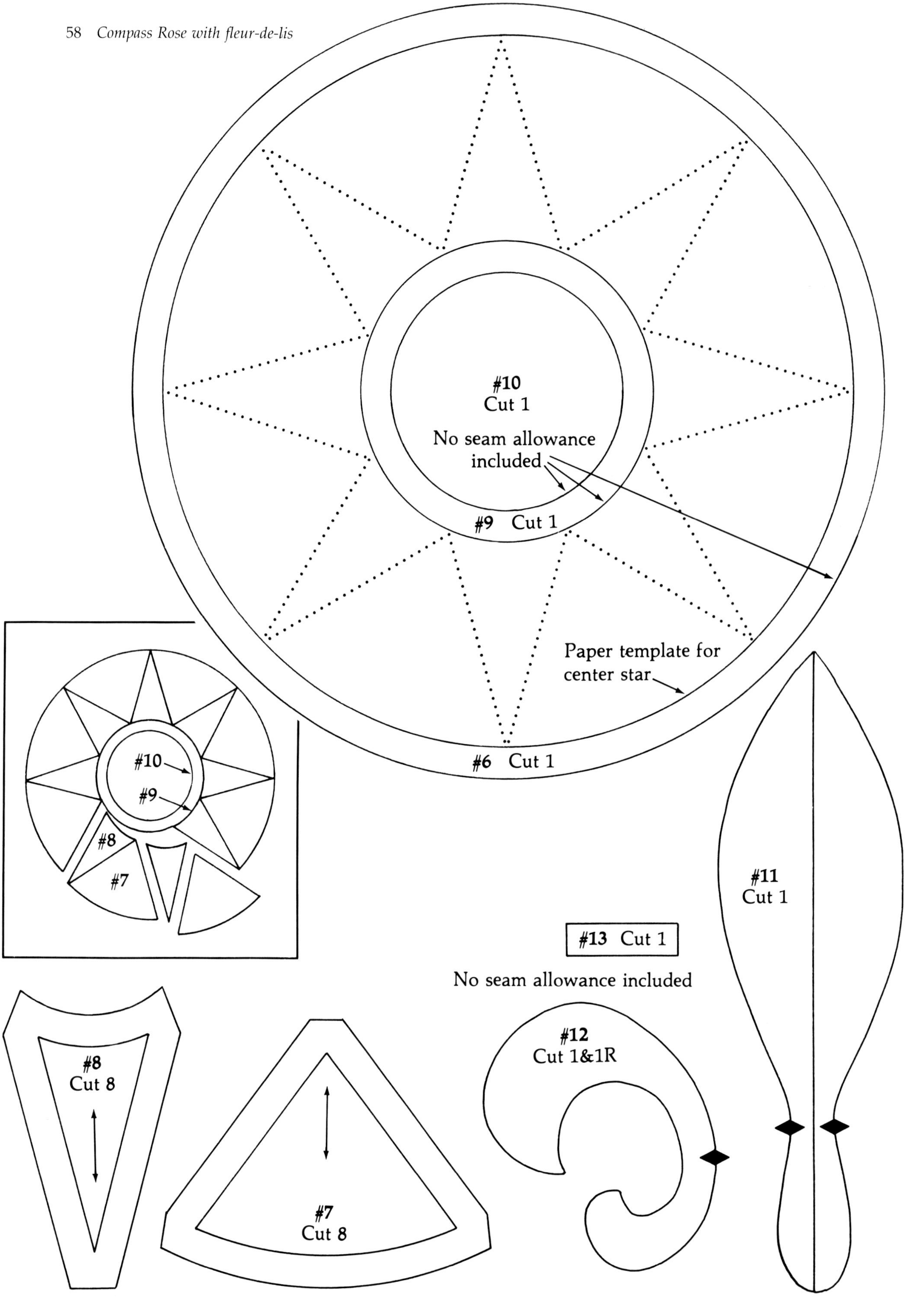

#10
Cut 1

No seam allowance
included

#9 Cut 1

Paper template for
center star

#6 Cut 1

#10
#9
#8
#7

#11
Cut 1

#13 Cut 1

No seam allowance included

#12
Cut 1&1R

#8
Cut 8

#7
Cut 8

Pattern 8

COMPASS AND STARS
16″ diameter for 18″ block

A hex sign on a placemat from a restaurant in Pennsylvania was the inspiration for this design. Piece the large star using the expanded piecing design with a "set-in" at the intersection of piece #1 and #1 reversed, and the inner star with sunburst variation piecing. The small stars are pieced into circles, basted to paper templates, and then appliquéd wherever you choose. Remove the fabric from behind the small star after it is appliquéd and press the seam allowances away from the circle as described in Chapter 4. Notice the different positions of the small stars in the upper left side of Nautical Stars (Color Plate 1) and the Fireworks wallhanging (Color Plate 8).

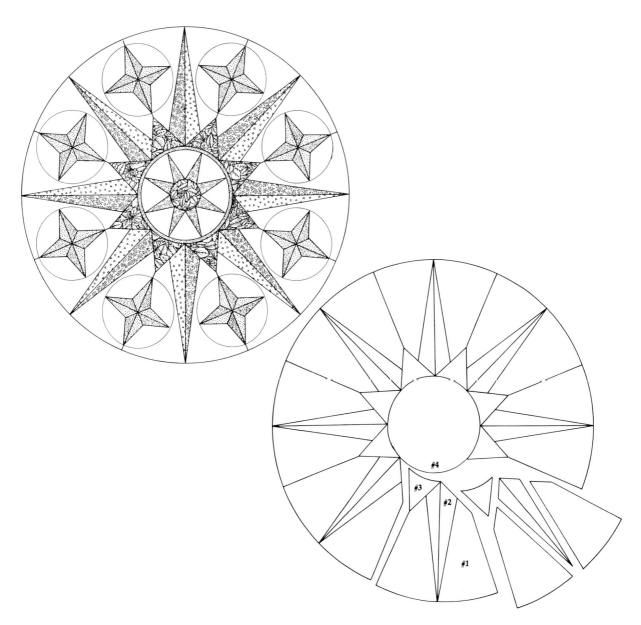

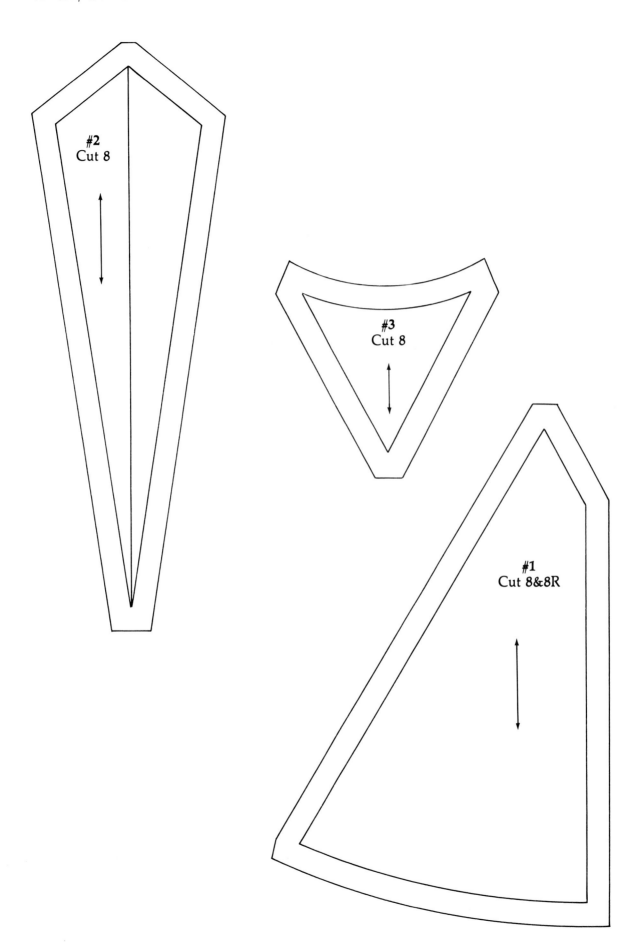

#2
Cut 8

#3
Cut 8

#1
Cut 8&8R

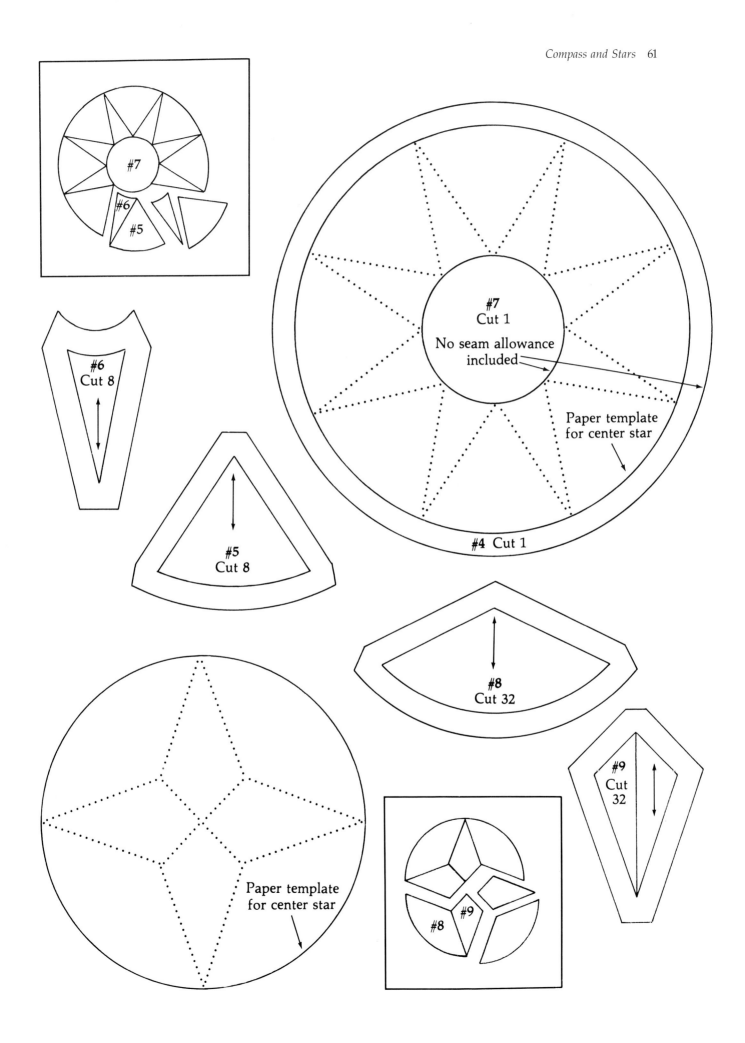

#7
Cut 1

No seam allowance
included

Paper template
for center star

#4 Cut 1

#6
Cut 8

#5
Cut 8

#8
Cut 32

#9
Cut
32

Paper template
for center star

Pattern 9

TWILIGHT STAR
30″ diameter

This is a simplified version of the star in the center of Nautical Stars. It could be used in the center of a medallion or nine of them would make a large quilt with an arrangement similar to the one in the quilt from the Shelburne Museum shown at the beginning of Part One. Use the general piecing instructions for the sunflower variation, plus the sunburst variation for the center small star. The background pieces for a circle this size are too large to present in this book. You can appliqué or piece into a large square as described in Chapter 4 or make a pattern for your own background quarters.

Draw a square one-quarter the size desired (example: 16″ square for 32″ background). Swing a yardstick compass from the corner to make an arc half the diameter of the Twilight Star (15″). Cut four pieces using this pattern (remember to add seam allowances).

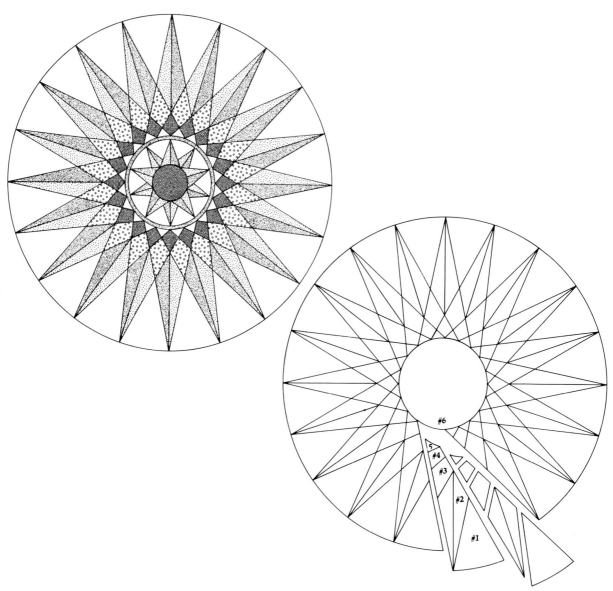

#3
Cut 20

#4
Cut 20

#2
Cut 20

#5
Cut 20

#1
Cut 20

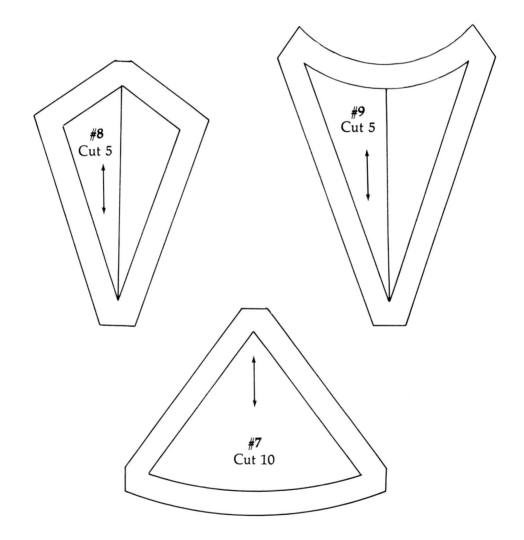

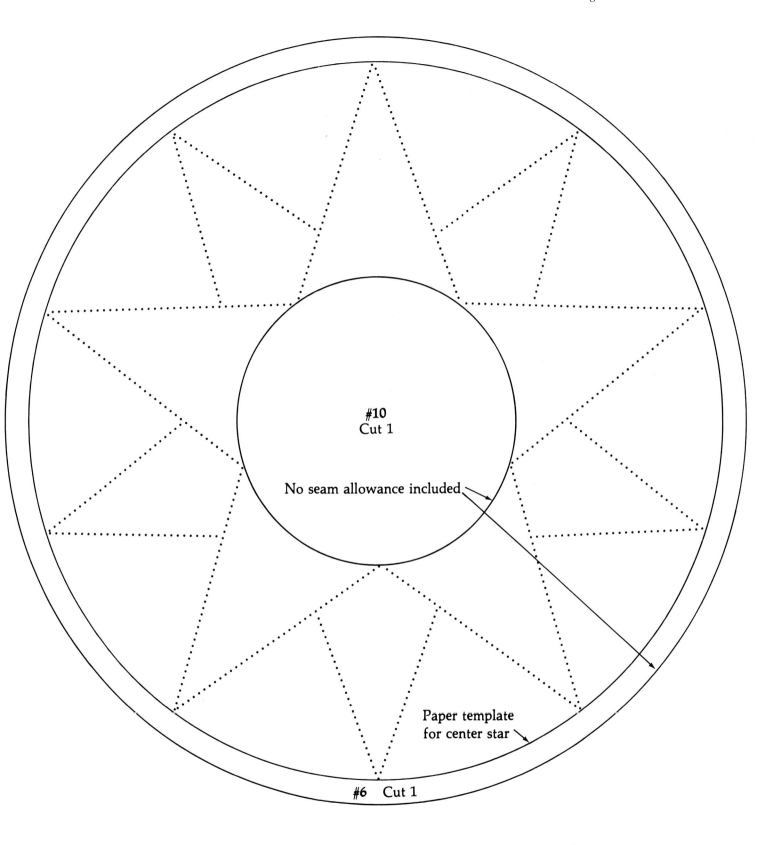

#10
Cut 1

No seam allowance included

Paper template
for center star

#6   Cut 1

Background Quarters for Patterns 1 through 8

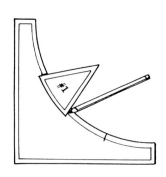

The patterns are given for all the designs
except Twilight Star.

INSTRUCTIONS
1. Fold tracing paper in half and trace the pattern.
2. Unfold to full size and glue it to template material.
3. Cut out four pieces. Use the piecing wedge pattern (#1) to make matching marks as illustrated.
4. Sew the four quarters together. Pin the Mariner's Compass design into the background quarters, using matching marks to position the points correctly, and stitch.

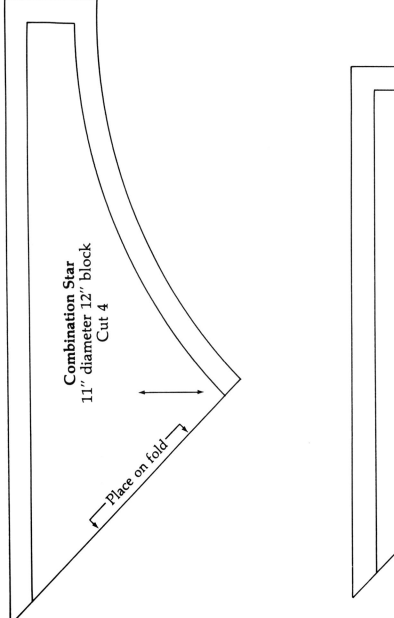

Combination Star
11" diameter 12" block
Cut 4

Place on fold

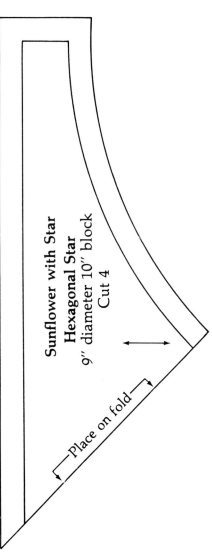

Sunflower with Star
Hexagonal Star
9" diameter 10" block
Cut 4

Place on fold

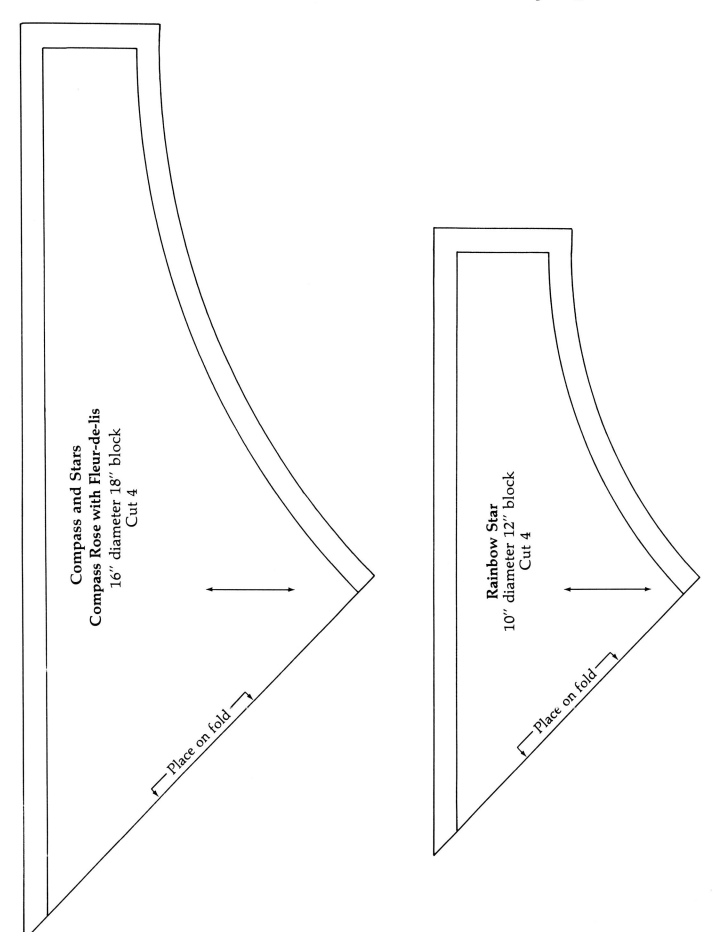

Compass and Stars
Compass Rose with Fleur-de-lis
16″ diameter 18″ block
Cut 4

Place on fold

Rainbow Star
10″ diameter 12″ block
Cut 4

Place on fold

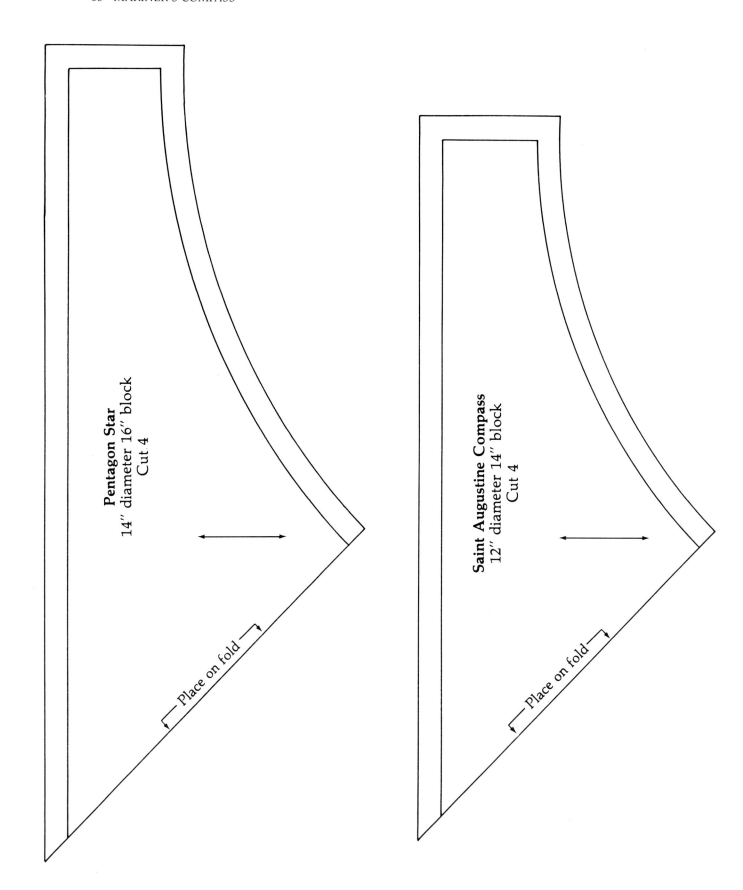

Pentagon Star
14″ diameter 16″ block
Cut 4

Place on fold

Saint Augustine Compass
12″ diameter 14″ block
Cut 4

Place on fold

Bibliography

An unnamed star from Nautical Stars quilt.

Beyer, Jinny. *Patchwork Patterns*. McLean, VA: EPM Publications, Inc., 1979.

Beyer, Jinny. *Medallion Quilts*. McLean, VA: EPM Publications, Inc., 1982.

Binney, Edwin, 3rd, and Binney-Winslow, Gail. *Homage to Amanda*. San Francisco: R. K. Press, 1984.

Brackman, Barbara. *An Encyclopedia of Period Quilt Patterns*. Lawrence, KS: 1981.

Carlisle, Lillian Baker. *Quilts at the Shelburne Museum*. Shelburne, VT: The Shelburne Museum, 1957.

"Compass." *Encyclopaedia Britannica*. 1944, p. 171.

Garoutte, Sally. *Uncoverings*. Mill Valley, CA: American Quilt Study Group, 1981.

"The Great American Quilt Classics: Mariner's Compass." *Quilter's Newsletter Magazine*. April 1980, p. 20.

Holstein, Jonathan. *The Pieced Quilt, An American Design Tradition*. Greenwich, CT: New York Graphic Society, Ltd., 1973.

Horton, Roberta. *Calico and Beyond*. Lafayette, CA: C&T Publishing, 1985.

Houck, Carter, and Miller, Myron. *American Quilts and How to Make Them*. New York: Charles Scribner's Sons, 1975.

Ickes, Marguerite. *The Standard Book of Quiltmaking and Collecting*. New York: Dover Publications, 1949.

Lipsett, Linda Otto. *Remember Me: Women and Their Friendship Quilts*. San Francisco: Quilt Digest Press, 1985.

McClosky, Marsha R. *Christmas Quilts*. Bothell, WA: That Patchwork Place, Inc., 1985.

Mosey, Caron. *America's Pictorial Quilts*. Paducah, Kentucky: American Quilter's Society, 1985.

Nelson, Cyril I. *The Quilt Engagement Calendar*. New York: E. P. Dutton, Inc., 1975, 1983, 1984, 1985.

Peto, Florence. *Historic Quilts*. New York: The American Historical Company, Inc., 1939.

Orlofsky, Patsy, and Orlofsky, Myron. *Quilts in America*. New York: McGraw-Hill Book Co., 1974.

Thompson, Silvanus Phillips. *Rose of the Winds: The Origin and Development of the Compass Card*. Proceedings, British Academy, London, England, 1913–1914.

Young, Blanche, and Young, Helen. *The Flying Geese Quilt*. Oak View, CA: Young Publications, 1983.

WHERE TO FIND OTHER MARINER'S COMPASS PATTERNS

Ardco Quilt Products, 131 Colvin Street, Rochester, NY 14511
  Metal templates for 18″ and 32″ Mariner's Compass and 12″ Storm at Sea.
Geary Associates, 5209 Portsmith Road, Fairfax, VA 22032
  Templates for 16″ round and 12″ × 16″ oval Mariner's Compass.
Judy Mathieson Designs, 5802 Jumilla Avenue, Woodland Hills, CA 91367
  Patterns for four 14″ round and one 14″ × 18″ oval Mariner's Compass.
Sterns Technical Textiles Company, Consumer Products Division, 100 Williams Street, Cincinnati, OH 45215–6316
  Sterns and Foster Catalog of Quilt Pattern Designs and Needlecraft Supplies.

BOOKS WITH MARINER'S COMPASS AND STORM AT SEA PATTERNS

Anthony, Catherine, and Lehman, Libby. *Sampler Supreme*. Santa Clara, CA: Leone Publishing Co., 1980. (Available from publisher, at 221 Main Street, Los Altos, CA 94022.)
  Book of 6″ blocks with two Mariner's Compass designs.
Martin, Judy. *Scrap Quilts*. Wheatridge, CO: Moon Over the Mountain Publishing Co., 1985. (Available from publisher, at 6700 West 44th Avenue, Wheatridge, CO 80033.)

To find COMPASS ROSE designs, look at maps, navigational charts, and books on the history of mapmaking in your public library.

BASIC QUILTMAKING BOOKS

Quilting, Patchwork, and Appliqué. Menlo Park, CA: Lane Publishing, 1981.
Leone, Diane. *The Sampler Quilt Book II*. Santa Clara, CA: Leone Publications, 1980.

QUILTING PERIODICALS

Lady's Circle Patchwork Quilts, Lopez Publications, 602 Montgomery Street, Alexandria, VA 22314–1576
Quilt Magazine, Harris Publications, 1115 Broadway, New York, NY 10010
Quilt World, P.O. Box 11304, Des Moines, IA 50340–1304
Quilter's Newsletter Magazine, P.O. Box 394, Wheatridge, CO 80034–0394

About the Author

Judy Mathieson began quiltmaking in 1973 and has been teaching in the Los Angeles area since 1977. She now teaches and lectures nationally and has designed and marketed patterns for quilts and quilted clothing.

A graduate of California State University, Northridge, she has served as a consultant on Judy Chicago's Dinner Party Project and as a collaborator with Betye Saar on the "Artist and the Quilt" exhibition. Her work has been included in the juried exhibition Quilt National several times and is often featured in quiltmaking publications.

Judy currently resides in Woodland Hills, California, with her husband, Jack. They have two sons.

Back Cover Photo: *Compass in a Storm.* Judy Mathieson and friends. 1984. 24″ × 29″. 6″ diameter compass. *Antique compass quilt.* Iowa. Circa 1880. 18″ diameter compass.

Other Fine Quilting Books from C & T Publishing:

A Celebration of Hearts
Jean Wells and Marina Anderson

An Amish Adventure
Roberta Horton

Baltimore Album Quilts: Historic Notes
and Antique Patterns
Elly Sienkiewicz

Baltimore Beauties and Beyond, Volume I
Elly Sienkiewicz

Boston Commons Quilt
Blanche Young and Helen Young Frost

Calico and Beyond
Roberta Horton

Contemporary Sampler
Katie Pasquini-Masopust

Crazy Quilt Handbook
Judith Montano

Crosspatch
Pepper Cory

Diamond Patchwork
Jeffrey Gutcheon

Fans
Jean Wells

Fine Feathers
Marianne Fons

Flying Geese Quilt
Blanche Young and Helen Young Frost

Friendship's Offering
Susan McKelvey

Heirloom Machine Quilting
Harriet Hargrave

Irish Chain Quilt
Blanche Young and Helen Young Frost

Landscapes and Illusions
Joen Wolfrom

Let's Make Waves
Marianne Fons and Liz Porter

Light and Shadows
Susan McKelvey

Mandala
Katie Pasquini-Masopust

Mariner's Compass
Judy Mathieson

New Lone Star Handbook
Blanche Young and Helen Young Frost

Perfect Pineapples
Jane Hall and Dixie Haywood

Picture This
Jean Wells and Marina Anderson

Plaids and Stripes
Roberta Horton

Quilting Designs From the Amish
Pepper Cory

Quilting Designs From Antique Quilts
Pepper Cory

Radiant Nine Patch
Blanche Young

Stained Glass Quilting Technique
Roberta Horton

Trip Around the World Quilts
Blanche Young and Helen Young Frost

Visions: Quilts of a New Decade
Quilt San Diego

Working in Miniature
Becky Schaefer

Wearable Art for Real People
Mary Mashuta

3 Dimensional Design
Katie Pasquini-Masopust

For more information write for a free catalog from:
C & T Publishing
P.O. Box 1456
Lafayette, CA 94553